Lydia's Journey

BOOK 1

Beginnings

JAMIE PHOENIX

Copyright © 2022 by Cristina Motatu-Stanescu

All rights reserved. No part of this book may be reproduced or used in any manner without written permission of the copyright owner except for the use of quotations in a book review.

First edition

In loving memory of Mica

Note from the author

Every human being on this planet has a story to tell, an experience to share, a question to ask. We come into this world with the purpose of experiencing life to the full and, more often than not, it turns out to be a series of challenging events – to say the least – meant to shape our understanding and perception of life.

Although it is certain that we are all born equipped with the same inner tools and resources, our life experiences are unique. Even though we are connected to one another through invisible threads of life energy, we all benefit from the free will in choosing one thought, one word, one action or one interaction – over another. And because of that, we each experience life in our own, unique way.

I have been hesitant to write this book because it may disturb the sensitivity of the reader in a number of ways. But then I had to consider that healing – both individually and collectively – comes through communication, and in some way, this book, as well as the following instalments in the Lydia's Journey series, have been written in the spirit of sharing and allowing. Sharing the pain and suffering of one human being. Allowing the healing through the journey of personal growth.

We have to be honest and brave if we are to commence our own healing process. It is a conscious decision, and it requires patience, persistence and, above all, love – of one's self. Only when we have learned to love and forgive ourselves, can we let go and begin anew.

My wish is that you will find it in yourself to love the wonderful person you are, and whatever your story, your experience, your question: be brave and curious, feel deeply into your heart and allow whatever wants to come forth to do so, for there is no journey of healing if you deny yourself the truth.

Jamie, January 2022

Acknowledgements

I have been blessed and privileged to be surrounded by many wonderful souls. I am deeply grateful to my dear friend Katie, who has been there for me from the word 'Dawn' and has constantly supported and encouraged me in the most loving way, which only a true friend can do.

I cannot forget Agi, who has nearly cried at some of the passages, and has been there for me with a kind word and a loving challenge, in my darkest moments of doubt.

The undeniable support and guidance throughout my own healing journey would not have been possible without the gentle and inspired assistance of my loving therapist, Julia.

And although you are not mentioned here by name, my love and gratitude go out to everybody with whom I have been in contact at some point in my life. Because each and every one of you has had a part to play in making this book possible.

After all, we are the painters as well as the painting in each other's lives.

Jamie, January 2022

Chapter 1

'We cannot change the past. We can only heal the past and in doing so, we become the best version of ourselves.'

Lydia, 2018

Dawn was approaching, yet the city was still asleep. The sky was turning in the east, above the sea, and the stars were beginning to fade as the daylight grew brighter. By the looks of it, the day was promising open skies and a cold winter temperature.

It was the 14th of December 2021, in a town on the eastern coast of Lincolnshire, England.

Lydia was sitting at her kitchen table, holding a steaming cup of coffee in her hands, daydreaming, letting her gaze brush the room in an almost detached stillness. She loved the early hours of the morning, when everybody in the house was still asleep, or barely waking up.

But this morning, sitting quietly at the table, she became suddenly and acutely aware that she was four days away

Lydia's Journey

from her fifty-fourth birthday and that this year, the celebration would not be the same as the last seventeen. She had never considered that a day would come when she would have to continue journeying alone through her life experiences.

She had recently separated from her husband and was getting ready for big changes in her life. Change of residence, change of career ... change in her relationship status.

Her world seemed to have turned upside down in the blink of an eye.

But Lydia was no stranger to change.

Ever since she could remember, there had been one constant theme in her life: change.

Lydia knew that actively changing her life would come from a moment of deep hurt, created from past beliefs, thoughts and emotions. One such moment could make the difference between the misery perpetuating itself or the shift designed to catapult her to who she was meant to be.

Whether she liked it or not, accepted it or not, Lydia knew that she was the creator of her own reality, and this time she would make sure that it would be what she had wanted to create from the beginning.

It was the year 1967. Lydia's parents, Harriet and Sergiu Munteanu lived in Bucharest, the capital of Romania.

Harriet had married young and in a hurry at the age of nineteen, because she was pregnant and Sergiu, six years older than her, was a prominent figure in his profession: a

Beginnings

musician, violoncello player, classical music teacher and composer. It would have been a shameful smudge on his prominent career if the news of him getting one of his students pregnant and then walking away had reached the press. He couldn't have that.

Harriet had been his private student for a couple of years before they got married and as far as Lydia had been told, Sergiu was the love of her mother's life.

She was visiting her parents in her hometown of Ploiesti, when her contractions started and her waters broke, so she had to be rushed to hospital and Harriet's mother Valery, who accompanied her daughter in the ambulance, was there when Lydia was born. In 1967 mobile phones did not exist so Harriet's father George was tasked with calling Sergiu from the house phone to let him know that his wife was in labour.

The day Lydia was born, a week before Christmas, the snow was falling slowly, in big fluffy flakes, covering the frosted ground with a white, soft blanket. It was the 18th of December, around 4 p.m.

'Oh, look at that precious little face, isn't she adorable!' whispered Valery, bending over Lydia's maternity crib, and picking her up to give her a closer look. Lydia was her first grandchild, and she knew that she would spoil her rotten.

'Yes, Mum, she is,' answered Harriet in an exhausted, almost annoyed voice.

The story of her birth was repeatedly told to Lydia, especially by her mother, even when she grew to be an adult. How Lydia, a healthy, red and wrinkly-looking baby girl, was born with her nose bent to one side of her face and not quite willing to cry – as you would expect newborns would do.

Year after year, Lydia listened to her mother recount how she was turned upside down by the doctor who helped deliver her, hanging by her feet, and how he had to give her a gentle slap on her bottom to make her take the first breath and cry. And Lydia did cry, dangling there upside down.

After all the wailing, Lydia realised that she was hungry, or thirsty. So, she cried again, but this time for food.

'What do you mean, you won't breastfeed her?' asked the midwife in uproar when Harriet made her announcement.

'I am not breastfeeding my daughter.'

And Harriet really meant it. She would not breastfeed her daughter, she stood her ground and she made it clear to anyone who would try to talk her into it.

'I will not do it.'

Years later, when Harriet decided to tell Lydia this story, she added, 'I was so brainwashed in those days, my dear, I didn't want to breastfeed you because your father told me that my breasts would sag if I did …'

Wow, don't you just love this total honesty? Even more so when you didn't ask for it?

But little Lydia was hungry, and thirsty, and scared because she could not feel her mother's nurturing touch, and she didn't care about the reason. She just wanted to be fed and feel safe.

Then, a Christmas miracle took place, when one of the new mothers from the same ward said to Harriet, 'Give her to me, my precious, I have enough milk for the both

Beginnings

of them. And she will be blessed in her life, you know, if she suckles at my breasts.'

This maternal, nurturing, young traveller woman had enough milk to help Lydia gain some weight so that she and her mother could leave the hospital on Christmas Eve.

The streets were covered in snow, the sky was heavy with clouds full of more snow, winter was well established, and people were getting ready for Christmas.

The festive period is a time to gather round in a warm house, surrounded by the people you love, sharing their stories from throughout the year. It was always magical for Lydia, she loved Christmas: the snow, Santa and his reindeer, the pine tree in her grandparents' living room spreading its fragrant scent throughout the house, the baubles shining through the needles, the traditional dishes, the baking, the hustle and bustle of families getting together in the kitchen, the hot cocoa, all the goodies being cooked on roaring fires ... Absolutely everything about Christmas delighted Lydia.

Her first Christmas was full of love and cheer, people holding her, hugging her, all those strangers smiling and talking to her in a goofy voice, she was the centre of their attention and the reason for their affections. Lydia was such a sweet and happy baby; she filled her grandparents' house with giggles and joy and their hearts with love. Even though her grandma seemed strict at times and heartless at others, and her granddad was often quiet or maybe did not pay Lydia as much attention as she wanted, she felt in her heart without an ounce of doubt that she was loved by them and she loved them back. They were her entire world.

Grandma Valery came from a big family, one of nine children her parents raised. She grew up in a big farmhouse in the countryside where her father planted and cultivated vineyards for the fruit and for wine making. She graduated in the city with an Art and Crafts bachelor's degree and she worked at a girls' secondary school, teaching them the art of textiles. She had fond memories of her pupils, even after so many decades, and the rug they had gifted her on her wedding day took pride of place in Valery's home.

After World War II ended the big political events across the world, and especially in Europe, shaped the face of countries as well as political and social interactions. Valery's family, like many others, were stripped of their possessions – land, assets and money in the bank – and forced into aligning with the ideology of the new political regime. Valery took the position of headteacher at the most popular nursery in town.

Valery met George, her husband, at a New Year's Ball, it was 1936 and she was twenty-two years old.

At that time, Europe was witnessing the rise of German power under the leadership of Adolf Hitler. But in Romania, for a young woman falling for a handsome and loving man, the rumours about a possible war in a faraway country were just that: rumours.

Lydia's grandfather was the only living child of his widowed mother. She dedicated her entire life to supporting her son and she saw him through his bachelor's degree in Accountancy, Granddad George worked as an accountant at one of the most well-known

Beginnings

firms in town. Valery was the only woman he knew. He fathered five children with Valery – the first two, unfortunately and to their despair, were not carried to term and the babies died prematurely in the womb. George and Valery suffered their loss terribly. They were devastated. Then, a third baby came along, a boy they named Kosta – he was healthy and noisy, just as babies are, the joy of their lives and a handful for both of them. A couple of years after Kosta was born, Marvin arrived, a healthy, blondish, curly-haired boy and some years later Harriet was delivered into this world, the long sought-after princess of their kingdom.

Lydia's first Christmas was a celebration for her extended family – not that she could remember, yet she was told that joy filled the home of George and Valery that day and friends and neighbours joined in the family's happiness.

Three weeks after Christmas, Harriet packed her bags, kissed her daughter goodbye, and went back to her place in Bucharest, a house deemed as being unsuitable for babies based on what Harriet would tell Lydia many years later.

Hours passed, days went on and weeks started to melt away her mother's memory. Lydia began to feel Grandma and Granddad were her parents, and the woman who came by once a week, or maybe once a month, became a visitor to her.

It's interesting how time can alter perception.

By the time Lydia was eight months old, a routine seemed to have formed in her daily life, another baby girl was sent to live with them for a little while – she had been born prematurely and needed the expert nurturing skills of her grandmother. This baby was Lydia's first cousin – Maribel.

Lydia loved Maribel's company, and the two girls enjoyed playing with one another..

Valery worked miracles with Maribel, and she basically saved her life. After several months, Maribel was thriving under the loving and persistent nurturing skills of her grandma.

Once Maribel started to grow and gain weight, becoming the beautiful, perfect, healthy baby she was meant to be, she and Lydia began to bond and it was not long before they were giggling and crawling together. Lydia would show off to Maribel, standing on two feet, and to her amusement her cousin would try to do the same.

As Maribel grew stronger she no longer lived with Lydia, she would go home with her parents and come back the next day.

It was a bit confusing for Lydia, at just two years old, to understand why she was living here and not with her parents, but whenever these thoughts and feelings arose Lydia learned to push them away and focus on what she did have – loving adults around who made her feel safe.

Lydia and Maribel shared not only their afternoons playing with their dolls or telling stories but also chickenpox and other similar childhood diseases.

Nursery years came along, and Lydia enjoyed being surrounded by other children. She also discovered that she had an auditory memory which enabled her to hold in her head all the roles in theatre plays she had seen, and she enjoyed secretly acting them out in her head as

Beginnings

her classmates were on stage, in front of their families at Christmas, year-end celebrations or festive occasions. Her teachers soon accepted Lydia's gift and more than once she would be called on to play several parts in the same show as she knew them all by heart.

During those happy years Lydia uncovered her competitive spirit – whenever there was a quiz at school where the winner was able to choose from a variety of professional outfits she was always determined to win the white coat and the toy stethoscope.

Her grandparents were extremely proud of Lydia's school achievements, and they realised that she might take the path of a university degree. So Valery, with her teaching background, used her skills to encourage Lydia to achieve her potential as the top of her class and the best student in the school.

When Harriet visited Lydia on the weekends, she would sometimes tell her daughter a story about a mama goat who went into town and bought carrots, cabbage, lettuce, apples, red peppers, green peppers, yellow peppers, round tomatoes, all sorts of vegetables for her little babies at home. The mama goat would carry all those goodies back home to her children, and when she got there she would knock at the door and ask her children to help her bring inside the carrots, cabbage, lettuce … until they got all the food in storage.

The story was narrated to a children's tune, with the purpose of encouraging memory skills through repetition. After listening to the same tale over and over again, Lydia finally said one day, 'Mama goat knocked at the door asking her children to help her out with *all her many veggies.*' After that, it was never mentioned again since Lydia had shown her summarising skills which rendered the purpose of the story moot.

One night Harriet came over, placed her suitcase next to the door, hugged and kissed Lydia then told her that she had to leave Romania, to follow Lydia's father to a place far away, in a different country. They would settle in and then they would come back for her.

'I will write to you daily, my dear,' said Harriet. Yet Lydia did not believe her.

'I will make sure you come to live with us, as a family, as soon as we get settled…' Again, Lydia felt the gap between the words and the meaning. For some reason, Lydia could not make much sense of her mother's remarks but she did fully understand the feeling of discomfort and unease that started to creep into her heart followed by a sense of loss. She wasn't sure what it was that she would lose, but she did feel it deep in her bones.

Then, as the night moved closer towards the day, everybody walked over to the train station in silence.

Her Uncle Marvin, Maribel's father, was trying to cheer them up with jokes but it all felt forced. There was sadness in the hearts of the adults, and this greatly unsettled Lydia.

Finally, in the darkness, they arrived and they waited on the dimly-lit platform until the train stopped.

Harriet stepped onto the carriage, put her suitcase down in the hallway and stood on the outdoor carriage stairs – travel safety measures being close to zero in those days. The train began its journey into the night with Lydia

Beginnings

on the platform of the empty station watching the train getting smaller and smaller and her mother waving at her before disappearing into the night.

There it was again, this sense of unease and discomfort, confusion and questions without answers.

Lydia turned to look at her grandma who was holding her hand tightly and saw some tears in the corner of Valery's eyes. Her grandad was standing next to Uncle Marvin, both exuding an air of inevitability and sadness. Only Maribel and her little brother John, seemed happy and oblivious to what was happening around them. Lydia decided that she would join them and ignore the adults.

She did not understand their sadness anyway. Her mother had come and gone ever since she could remember, and she saw nothing special about Harriet leaving that night on the train.

Lydia was four years old when her mother and father relocated abroad leaving her behind in the care of her grandparents.

Days passed, months disappeared, a full year slipped by and Lydia was still living with her grandparents. This would be her home; this would definitely be her place, she thought.

Once in a while, Valery showed Lydia pictures of her mother. Lydia vaguely remembered her, but she became just a black and white image of a woman on a piece of paper, attached to the handwritten letters which arrived maybe once a month.

Lydia and her grandparents lived in a detached house in a quiet neighbourhood in the city, with a garden spacious enough for a tall and shady tree from which Lydia's swing hung, half a metre from the ground. For a while, Lydia's great grandmother, Ana, lived with them, she was George's mother. She was a bit deaf, but Lydia liked to play outside with Ana watching from her chair under the tree.

Lydia had heard the story about her granddad's upbringing many times. At the end of World War I when the soldiers started return home, Ana, who had not heard news of the fate of her husband who had been sent to the front line, started a journey on foot through the Balkans to find him, taking her four children with her. It was the beginning of winter 1918. During the voyage, she lost three of her children due to illness – typhus – and by a miracle, her fourth child, George, was saved from death. She found the remains of her husband and brought his body back to be buried in holy ground in his family town. After that, it was said that Ana, a young, widowed mother of striking beauty, had many suitors yet she did not want to marry any of them until years later, when she accepted in matrimony a rich farm owner from her home town, whose wife died of illness, leaving behind three children. Ana was moved by his circumstances and could relate to the loneliness of a single parent so she decided that she would accept his proposal and they got married. For a while, the story talks of her and her new family being happy. The children grew up together, moved on and started their own families, and when her second husband died she moved in with her son and his new wife, Valery, and their family.

Lydia and Great Grandma Ana were buddies. Sometimes, Lydia would climb on her bike and go up and down the alley leading from the main gate to the front door. Ana would sit at the side and wave to Lydia, pretending

Beginnings

that she was riding on a real road, and she would need assistance to cross it. It was fun for both of them, and Lydia couldn't get enough of the game.

Her grandparents were pious people, they followed the teachings of the orthodox church and observed its rituals.

When Lydia was five years old, her grandma introduced her to Jesus, his love for and in the hearts of men and women, and, of course, the church, the house where Jesus lived.

But no matter how much attention she paid to everything going on in that church, during the service, Lydia could never see Jesus, I mean in person. Only in paintings. Nevertheless, there was something special about church. There was a feeling of safety and comfort, pretty similar to what Lydia felt in her grandparents' home.

At first, going to church felt like a drag, all those people around her, sitting still, listening, then standing up, forming lines of women on one side and men on the opposite side, all those rituals, those songs – Lydia didn't really get it.

Once she remembered standing in those queues with her grandma, waiting behind other women to move, it was in the wintertime, she was wearing a white full cover hat and a red coat – as red was Lydia's favourite colour – and all of a sudden, she smelt fire coming from somewhere nearby and heard the shrill of a woman's voice.

'She's burning! Her hat … look at her hat … it's burning!'

Lydia started to feel people pounding her, slapping her hard on her head and shouting at her.

'Stand still, child! Your hat is burning, stand still!'

What a commotion, goodness gracious!

Lydia's Journey

Obviously, Lydia was saved. The hat was ruined, and hopefully, some learned that day to keep distance from people's heads when holding a burning candle.

After that, going to church felt unsafe and still a chore. And yet, her grandma insisted, and Lydia had to attend every Sunday.

So she went, week after week, by the hand of her grandma, sat down, listened to the songs, watched other people pray, got lost in her own world. It started to feel safe again and comforting. So Lydia decided to stop resisting it in her heart.

By now she had given up on looking for Jesus. It was obvious he did not want to meet all these people gathered around, but it was also obvious to her that he didn't mind them coming and going in a place that was said to be his home. The more Lydia paid attention to the melody in the songs, the more she started to enjoy this place and in her lilting voice, she sang along and had fun with the rituals.

One day, Lydia came to the realisation that Jesus is not a person, Jesus is a feeling that people are searching for, and she felt in her heart something that she could not explain. From that moment on, Lydia knew it without a doubt: it was home.

Home means many things to many people; to Lydia it meant love and safety, where one can be who they want, think without judgement, feel and express their humanness.

Lydia never confided this secret to anyone. Yet she would feel peace in her heart, throughout her life, whenever she chose to and it turned out to be her life saver, literally.

Beginnings

One spring day, Lydia was playing outside in the garden. She felt great in the sunshine, life was buzzing around her, and she had a sense of joy and safety and love. For reasons that she could not remember when asked later, she opened the gate of her grandparents' front garden, walked out onto the street, and dashed across the road, in front of a moving car!

Years after that, whenever she remembered that day, she could not understand or explain what had possessed her to do such a thing. Maybe it was the thrill of danger that launched her? Or perhaps it was just that she saw something on the other side of the road, and she felt curious, she wanted to explore? Who could know?

Lydia survived the experience, although the car squeaking its brakes and the driver shouting and swearing wasn't exhilarating at all. She did not feel like a superhero after all! In fact, that incident had serious consequences in the form of several days of being housebound and not allowed to play outside and, of course, some smacking of her bottom.

Lesson learned: no more dashing in front of cars. Not even in front of those that are standing still – because you can never tell.

⁓

Lydia took a long sip from her steaming coffee cup. The sun was rising, and the light began to slide into the room through the kitchen windows. A smile formed at the corners of her lips and a warm feeling attached to those early memories found its way into her heart.

⁓

Lydia's Journey

Just before Lydia started primary school her grandparents decided to move, from the family home into a one-bedroom apartment. Lydia did not know the reason behind this change but she visited the construction site a couple of times, with Granddad George, to observe the progress of the apartment building.

Ana had died before they moved into the new apartment. Lydia missed her deeply and it took a while for her to understand and accept that when somebody is said to have passed away it meant she would never see them again.

When they finally moved into the new place it felt crowded. The rooms were small.

Lydia had no bedroom of her own, she had to sleep in the corner of her grandparents' bed. The apartment had no garden, only a small balcony attached to the bedroom, where her grandma grew pots of plants and herbs.

The living room was also her after school homework room, where she sat at an old, black wooden piece of furniture which resembled both a bookcase and an extendable writing desk. Her feet didn't even touch the ground when she sat at it. Lydia remembered how they used to dangle during her long hours of daily homework.

But there was something great about this new place: it was on the first floor of a four-storey apartment building, with other similar buildings around, some taller, with many other families with children her age.

This was just too good to be true! Lydia couldn't wait to make new friends.

If she behaved at home, got good grades in school and finished all her homework on time, she was allowed to go outside and play with all the other kids.

Beginnings

Lydia started every afternoon with the same goal: to do what she was told as best she could so that she could go outside and play.

Some afternoons, her homework was a breeze, while other days she sat at her desk for hours on end, rewriting the same passages over and over again until she got them just the way her grandma wanted: perfect.

Lydia remembered how one afternoon, Grandma Val had to attend a parents' evening meeting at school, leaving Lydia in the care of her granddad.

'Easy peasy' muttered Lydia to herself with an ever-so-slight smile raising the corners of her mouth in anticipation of a playful afternoon outdoors. Little did she know that Valery had left George strict instructions about the expectations regarding Lydia's homework: perfection. And perfection was indeed the reason Lydia was still sitting at her desk that evening when Valery arrived home.

For many years to come, Lydia's school journey would be all about perfection, regardless of who was in charge of her.

Lydia made friends easily. They all played chasing games, war games, ball games, digging-holes-in-the-ground games …

One afternoon Lydia and her friends, two other girls around her age and living in the buildings close by, climbed up a pile of dirt which appeared to have been left behind by the construction team who had dug out the foundations of a new building behind Lydia's block. It resulted in quite a high elevation, maybe three times

Lydia's Journey

Lydia's height. Lydia had an idea: they could turn it into a private cave and if they dug deep and wide enough they could all fit inside. It would be an awesome hiding place during their other adventures, and Lydia suggested that they start digging as soon as they gathered some tools.

It was near the end of the summer and it was still hot at midday. They started working on their 'cave' and soon it became quite obvious that it was going to take more than just the couple of days they had anticipated. The 'mountain' was full of broken bricks and stones, and they had to be careful because sometimes they would step on pieces of broken glass and sharp metal shards. The girls tried to keep their project to themselves but it drew attention and soon word about their actions spread. The 'cave digging' project, became a strategic element in their collective war game and that pile of rubble transformed into their fortress. They had managed to carve a hole waist deep. They realised it would not be safe to continue digging further than that as they had not figured out how to prevent the ceiling from falling in on them.

Lydia loved being included in this group, she liked the feeling of belonging. Some afternoons while she was waiting for her friends to come out to play, she would walk around the manicured front yards of the building and pick red flower petals to stick to her fingernails, because Lydia was, after all, also a little lady who loved long, painted fingernails and trinkets, shiny baubles on her fingers and around her wrists and neck.

She made a promise to herself one afternoon, as she was applying the petals to her fingers, and she knew that she would keep it because Lydia was a person who honoured her commitments: 'When I grow up to be a woman, I will always have my fingernails looked after and polished.'

Beginnings

The first day of primary school arrived, and Lydia stood in the crowd gathered in the schoolyard, with her grandma next to her.

'You're going to be all right, my darling,' whispered Valery in her ear. 'You will make new friends and your teacher will be there if you need anything.' Although it sounded reassuring, Lydia still felt the butterflies lurking inside her tummy.

She was wearing her brand-new uniform, all cleaned and pressed, looking like a proper schoolgirl on her first day.

Grandma guided her gently towards a tall woman standing at the doorway of the massive building. She was smiling broadly at the new arrivals and when her pupils gathered round, she introduced herself as Miss Laura Petrescu, teacher of class C.

'Off you go, Lydia dear, follow your teacher and do as you are told, and I'll be here waiting for you at the end of the day.' Valery watched Lydia walk away with Miss Laura and the rest of her flock.

They went down a long corridor, turned some corners then finally reached a classroom where they all got to pick their seats. Being the first day, they each had to introduce themselves, talk about where they lived, their parents and what they did for a living, their siblings if they had any.

The children were all very well-mannered and none dared to speak without being asked to. When Lydia's turn arrived and she started talking about her grandparents, her life with her cousins and the extended family, her parents living abroad. A sense of discomfort grew in her as Miss Laura interrupted, seeming irritated.

'That will be all, Lydia, thank you,' she said abruptly, and Lydia came to a full stop in her story.

Lydia's Journey

The day finished, Lydia walked out of the classroom and ran to the exit to meet her grandma. Close behind was Miss Laura, walking stiffly and swiftly, she wanted a word with Valery.

After a short conversation with the teacher, Valery took Lydia's hand in hers, bent over gently to stroke her hair and gave her a kiss on the forehead.

'Let us walk back home, my dearest, and you can tell me all about your very first day at school,' she said as they left the school grounds.

Grandma didn't seem to be annoyed with her so Lydia stopped worrying, the world was making sense again.

A week later, Lydia was introduced to a different teacher, Miss Ana Raducanu of class B, a slender, middle-aged woman who gently took Lydia's hand in hers and introduced her to her new classmates.

Lydia liked it better here. The children seemed friendlier, and Miss Ana was all smiles when she addressed them. There was an air of kindness about her, and Lydia decided that she liked her better than Miss Laura.

Not long after this lucky turn of events, Lydia learned from eavesdropping on her grandparents' conversations that Miss Laura did not like Lydia being in her class, because of her parents living abroad.

For crying out loud! What kind of nonsense is that?

Well, at that time there was a wall in Berlin, built in 1961 by the Soviet authorities stationed in Germany post-World War II. This wall, known as the Berlin Wall, divided Germany into a democratic western country and a socialist one in the east. It represented the psychological and ideological division between the East and the West,

Beginnings

where the Eastern European countries were ruled by socialist parties approved by the Soviet authorities, and the Western European ones were led by democratically-elected governments.

Lydia lived in an Eastern European country governed by an ever-vigilant Communist Party who told people how to think and what opinions were acceptable. Her parents, on the other hand, lived in the Federal Republic of Germany, the western territory, a country where people felt free to express their views. Back then, if you lived in Eastern Europe, it was entirely unacceptable to desire the freedom of expression, to have an opinion that was not in compliance with the Communist Party's guidelines. Wanting to live or being related to someone living in a democratic country was considered treason by many, at least in public, and it was wise to walk away from such people and avoid any associations with them.

Miss Laura was simply too afraid to deal with such a treasonous family and didn't want the rest of her pupils to be 'estranged from the truth and lost in the land of perdition by Lydia's background.'

And this is how Lydia learned what a hideous thing her parents had apparently done and yet, she felt it again, the gap between the words and the meaning.

Lydia liked going to school. Miss Ana sat her in the front row, and she soon became close friends with several of her classmates; she wished Maribel was there with her, but Maribel lived in a different part of town, so she went to another school.

It didn't matter that much though because Lydia and Maribel would see each other every day after school at

Lydia's Journey

Grandma's, where Maribel was sent to do her homework.

Each day, they sat at the kitchen table, eating their lunch, then they would go to take a nap with Grandma – which they both hated – after which they sat at their desks and studied. It was so tempting to just put down their pencils and chat!

On one occasion, they concocted a plan to skip the afternoon nap. They had to make sure Grandma would not be woken by the girls sneaking out of the bed they all slept in, so Lydia told Maribel to be patient and wait for Lydia to make it out of bed first. There they were, both waiting for Grandma to fall asleep. When they heard that soft, regular snore, Lydia made the first move, slowly, very slowly, sliding down to the edge of the bed. She was fully aware of how light her grandmother's sleep was … so she moved and paused and moved again, painfully slow. It seemed to take forever to move across one metre of bedsheets and blankets, yet she made it! She felt the edge with her feet and started to get a bit impatient. Yet she kept it steady and managed to sit herself up. And she was just about to get up when she heard, 'Lydia, nap time isn't over yet, go back to bed!' That was impossible, Lydia told herself, how did Grandma manage to catch that?

Many afternoons later, after about just as many attempts, Lydia and Maribel did manage to sneak out of the bed and have a little play time before Grandma woke up. Victory!

Ah, what good times those were.

Another time, they were both doing their homework and when Grandma came to check on them, Lydia suddenly noticed a commotion behind her, coming from Maribel's desk. When she turned around to see what was happening, she couldn't help but stare at the scene.

Beginnings

'Maribel, stand still I say, and look at the mess you've made on those pages. That's messy handwriting, I'm telling you! Now, you go back and do it again!'

'No, I won't!'

'Yes, you will.'

'No, I WON'T!' said Maribel as she broke free from Valery's grip and put some distance and the dining table between them.

Grandma was first shocked, then furious.

'How dare you! Come back here!'

But Maribel was determined to keep her distance, so Grandma had to make the first move around the table.

Grandma came closer, Maribel moved away, and soon they were both running around the table in a chase.

'Lydia!' shouted Valery with a grunt, 'Lydia, stop her, grab her!'

But Lydia was no fool. She would not get in between them; she would not take sides. Besides, it was so much fun to watch them both running around that table!

Soon after that incident, Maribel stopped coming to Grandma's house in the afternoon for homework and although she was never told the reason Lydia had an idea as to why the arrangement had changed.

It felt lonely for a while, and it was no longer funny to try and sneak out of the bed, so Lydia ended up falling asleep with Grandma during the afternoon nap.

School was a happy place to be. Grandad George stopped taking Lydia to school after the first few weeks, when he realised that he couldn't walk very far without his nitroglycerine tablets. After a couple of mornings of him barely keeping up with the pace, he and Valery decided that Lydia was old enough to go to school by herself – she was nearly seven years old. To encourage and reassure Lydia in that she was a grown-up girl, Grandma gave her a duplicate set of house keys which Lydia held with pride, tight on a string around her neck, underneath her school uniform. It was a big moment for Lydia, she had been entrusted with the house keys, and it felt great.

School days blended into one another and soon the winter break arrived bringing with it Lydia's favourite holiday: Christmas. This year, in her new role as a responsible granddaughter, Lydia wanted to give her grandma a surprise gift. She knew exactly what it would be and how to acquire it, Lydia had a piggy bank, in the shape of Santa's boot, full of coins waiting to be put to a good use.

One afternoon, while her grandparents were busy in the kitchen, Lydia decided to act. For some time now she had been looking at a clay bird in the farmers' market through which she walked every morning on the way to school and she thought of her grandma Val, how she would like that bird, how she would fill it up with water and then blow into it to make it sing … Lydia smiled at the scene in her head and she decided that she would buy that bird. She picked up her piggy bank and looked for a way to take the money out. The only way was to cut it open. She took her school scissors from her bag and diligently started cutting into the plastic of the boot. It proved to be a very challenging and complicated task, cutting through hard plastic, but that did not deter Lydia from achieving her goal. She put all her effort, strength and attention, not to mention sticking out her little tongue in the process, maybe that way it would be done sooner,

Beginnings

and after several long minutes of perseverance Lydia finally opened the piggy bank and started taking out the coins. How am I going to take the money out of the house tomorrow? Lydia asked herself, realising that she would not have a moment alone in the morning and that her grandma would check her pockets to make sure that Lydia had everything packed for school before she left the apartment.

She started thinking and looking around until she finally decided that the best hiding place for the coins was her mittens. But the mittens were in her coat and her coat was hanging in the hallway, next to the kitchen, and her grandparents were in the kitchen talking, and the kitchen door was open … gosh, why was this all so complicated?

Well, there was no other way but to sneak into the hallway and be as quiet as possible.

So, she did just that. Luckily, adults don't always pay attention to the little noises around them, so Lydia had the mittens, had the coins, and now just needed to put her plan into action tomorrow.

The next morning, Lydia got ready for school as usual, secretly giggling inside at the prospect of her surprise. She kissed her grandma goodbye, turned around, and put her bare hand on the door handle ready to turn it.

'Lydia, your gloves, sweetheart, you have to put your gloves on before you get out there in the cold,' said Grandma.

'I'll do that in a minute, just let me open the door.'

That didn't go down well with Valery, her protective mama bear senses detected something out of sorts in

Lydia's Journey

Lydia and she made her turn around and pull the mittens out of her pockets.

There was no way Lydia could have just disappeared, mittens or no mittens.

So, she did as she was told and two, fully stuffed mittens were presented to grandma who looked at them in amazement, before hell broke loose and drama ensued.

Grandma was furious, but she had to let Lydia go because she was already running late. After school Lydia didn't want to go home. Grandma was waiting and Lydia was at a loss. But she went back, dragging her feet, and she stood there in front of a stern set of grandparents who told her all she needed to know about deceit, and falsehood, and stealing money.

'I wasn't stealing money! That money was mine, given to me, for my piggy bank.' She felt a little emboldened by the surprise on their faces, but it didn't last long, and they disregarded her statement and reinforced the lesson about asking for permission before acting.

'I just wanted to give you a gift, Grandma, that's why I took my money out,' said Lydia, finally giving up on defending her actions and understanding that she would not win this one.

Thinking back to the incident now, Lydia realised that it might have been the first time she felt disappointed in her grandparents, especially her grandma.

By the time Valery finally calmed down and understood Lydia's intention, the spirit in which it was conceived was gone, spoiled, ruined, impossible to mend and Lydia

Beginnings

learned not to give gifts without prior approval. Which is in its essence ironic.

Her grandparents wanted somehow to make it right and a couple of weeks into the new year, they sat Lydia down and told her that if she finished her first year of school at the top of her class, they would buy her a bike – a real, big kids' bicycle.

This caught Lydia by surprise. She had really wanted to have one – since forever.

So, the deal was on. She could not miss out on this opportunity.

She did have a desire to learn, and she also had a competitive spirit. The promise of this bicycle just sparked her talents and gave her a strong motivation to finish first.

Around the beginning of February, a letter arrived from her parents, letting the whole family know that Lydia's baby brother had been born, and her mother sent pictures of herself smiling and holding a little creature in her arms. They had named him Liviu, and they said he was as cute as pie. They also mentioned in a footnote that they wished Lydia was there to enjoy this new arrival.

Lydia felt she was where she belonged, she did not feel the need to be anywhere else and when the celebrations for the new arrival died down, she put the joyous news behind her.

At the end of her first year in school, there was to be a public assembly in the schoolyard – apparently they had one every year – in which the names of the first, second and third ranking pupils were called out and they would climb onto a podium to receive their certificates and the gifts attached to each place.

That year turned out to be a first in the history of Lydia's school, because there were five winners of the first prize in her class. And Lydia was one of them.

She was so happy. And a bit scared, or shy, not sure that she wanted to stand there in front of the entire school, teachers, parents and grandparents, to receive her certificate and the gift of a couple of novels.

Just think of your bike, soon you'll get your bike, and you can go outside and show it to all your friends, she reminded herself as she climbed up the stairs to take her place in the school's history.

Everything went well, everybody was happy, Lydia and her classmates said goodbye to each other for the summer break, and they all walked home.

Lydia was chirpy, Grandma was proud, and the anticipation of the moment was just too sweet. Grandad was waiting for them when they arrived at the apartment. He gave Lydia a big hug and looked at her with a soft smile on his face. Lydia liked to see him smile. He was a quiet, gentle person and Lydia loved him very much.

But she didn't want to ruin the moment and she knew better than to ask, so she waited patiently for her gift to show up.

Finally, her grandparents sat her down. 'We are so very proud of you, Lydia. We know that you have worked hard to finish top of your class, as did the others. We promised you a bicycle, and we consulted with your parents, and they wrote back to us saying that it would be OK with them if you promise to be careful … And then we thought

Beginnings

about the risks of you being out there, on your bike, in the street, and realised that we have the responsibility of your upbringing for as long as you are under our care …'

Lydia started to think that they were using way too many words for giving a gift when all she wanted was for them to just pull out the bike from the balcony. *What's that talk about my parents?* she wondered. *They're not here? What do they have to do with my bike?* Suddenly a chill went down her spine. *Are they telling me that I won't get the bike? No, that's just not possible, they promised …*

Her grandparents were still talking when Lydia pulled herself out of her thoughts and back into their long speech, '… .and we know we promised you the bicycle, but we think now that it wasn't a responsible thing to suggest so, instead, we got you this lovely … plush dog.'

Oh my God, hell open and just take me! was all that Lydia could think. She looked at her grandparents, then at the toy in her hand, then back at her grandparents. She stood there looking, and feeling, stupid. And betrayed. And utterly disappointed.

It was too much for her to deal with. She pushed the feeling down, into that dark corner of her heart where she stored all those painful and uncomfortable moments, hoping that she would never feel like that again.

The joy, the pride, the accomplishment, all tied up in a stupid bike which was never meant to be.

The promise that was not honoured, was so hurtful that Lydia didn't know how to deal with it without making her grandparents angry. After all, they were looking at her waiting to see her joy at receiving the cuddly dog.

All Lydia could do in that moment was smile. So she did.

Lydia's Journey

And so, the summer began. Lydia played outside with her friends, she took a two-week trip to the beach with her grandparents and spent all the time she could with Maribel and her little brother John. And soon, like everything else in life, that moment of mixed emotions passed, the summer came and went and there she was, back in school and ready to start over again.

Year two of primary school started, and Lydia decided to concentrate on her grades with no need for recognition other than the prize at the end of the school year and climbing up the stairs of the podium.

It happened and Lydia was proud. This time there was no disappointment, no expectations, no broken promises. And Lydia liked the fact that she could fully enjoy her first prize this year.

Then it was summer again. The break was great, they went to her grandparents' favourite vacation place, where they went every year and where Lydia met with her holiday friends.

It was a coastal city, full of nice boulevards, green, shady parks, hot sands on the beach and dark blue sea waters.

The three-hour trip to get there was full of fun and drama, Lydia, her grandma, granddad and Maribel, all bundled up and squeezed into the back seat. The car belonged to her colourful great uncle and aunt, Grandma's sister and brother-in-law, both in their early sixties. The stories they told, the fun they had, the way they were prodding one another as they took turns behind the wheel turned Lydia's summer breaks with them into a hilarious adventure.

Beginnings

Uncle Mihai was a retired engineer who had served in World War II as a pilot. He had seen and lived experiences that are now part of humanity's dark memories. He had been in prison after the war ended, by the decision of a communist judge and in accordance with the new government who considered educated people to be a threat to society, thus they needed to be forced into compliance or killed. Pretty much as Stalin did when he came to power in the Soviet Union. As Uncle Mihai had a university degree, he was sent to do work on the dams during his imprisonment. He had lost so much weight during those years that he left prison a shadow of the man he once was, with second degree muscular wastage. He told Lydia many years later that he had sworn to himself never to go hungry again for as long as he may live, which is why, ever since Lydia could remember him, Uncle Mihai was rather on the large size for his height.

Auntie Mara reminded Lydia of an aristocrat of old. She loved to wear white shell bracelets and necklaces during the summer because they would contrast nicely with her tanned skin. Stories from her youth concerned her beauty and high performance in her studies. She was a retired lawyer, and she looked and talked like one – in firm and concise sentences, with an authoritarian tone. But Lydia didn't mind the tone, nor the authority, Grandma Val and Auntie Mara were pretty similar on that account. Auntie Mara had been married to someone else before Uncle Mihai, she spoke about him a lot and his picture was still in her living room. Lydia understood and sensed the deep connection and regrets of her aunt when she talked about her first husband. He had died of a stroke and her aunt had witnessed it. It was a sad story told often at family gatherings.

Lydia's Journey

Lydia loved Auntie Mara and Uncle Mihai.

The trip was entertaining, and they stopped often to swap the driver and take short breaks. They ate outdoors, at the same restaurant on their way there and back, at a table under large, magnificent, old acorn trees. The food was always delicious, they ate the local delicacy *mititei*, which were similar to sausage rolls but juicier, dipped in plenty of mustard and washed down with cold and fizzy lemonade. Lydia loved the way they sat, and chatted, and ate and had fun together. The entire atmosphere was of ease and joy. At home, during the school period, Lydia felt pressure and demands. Here, sitting at the table under the trees, she felt free of worries, enjoying herself and the company.

The beach they visited nearly every summer was always crowded, and Lydia had to get to the shore navigating through beach towels and bodies toasting in the sun, so close to each other that a needle could be dropped without touching the sand. It was frustrating and some days Lydia didn't even bother, she would spend time in the shade of the wall where they would place their towels.

Going to the beach in the mornings was a sacred ritual. Each evening one of the adults of their group assumed responsibility to go to the beach before sunrise the next day and pick the best spot, preferably near the tall wall which would cast a nice, protective shadow at midday. The designated person would wake up with the roosters and walk down to the beach, spread out the towels to reserve their space and then wait for the others.

The rest of the group woke up a little after dawn, had breakfast, packed the bags and headed over to the beach. If the group was bigger than two families then more than one adult would go early. There were a lot of towels.

Beginnings

They spent most of the day on the beach. After the sun finally started to set, they packed up and made their way back to their lodgings, they washed out the sand and then got ready for a short walk along the promenade before dinner.

Some days, if the air was too hot, they left the beach before lunch and took refuge under the old trees bracing the terraces of the bars, overlooking the sea. Then they walked through town, and stopped to buy corn on the cob. Lydia loved the corn boiled in its own leaves, it burst under her bite, spreading its very sweet flavour onto her tastebuds. Then they headed back to their rooms to rest.

Some nights they all went to the outdoor movie theatre. Popcorn, soft breeze and funny movies, what could be better than that?

Other evenings, they went to an outdoor restaurant for a meal followed by ice cream. Delicious!

One night at dinner Lydia was sitting next to Uncle Mihai. It was dessert time and Lydia finished hers quickly then sat there, listening and watching the adults. Uncle Mihai bent over to her and asked, 'Would you like to go see if you can find that bracelet you showed me earlier?'

Lydia's eye sparkled. She did not think her uncle had paid attention to that but he had.

She nodded quickly and they got up to leave the table.

'Where are you two going?' asked Valery.

'Oh, we're just stretching our legs,' answered Uncle Mihai.

Then someone asked Valery a question and she turned back to the conversation leaving them alone.

Uncle Mihai even remembered where the stall with the

sparkling plastic bracelets and rings and necklaces was. Lydia picked up the bracelet she liked, gave Uncle Mihai a big, effusive hug and put the precious treasure on her left wrist.

When they arrived back at the table, of course, her grandma noticed the bracelet and shook her head but it was summer after all, and little luxuries were allowed.

Fair warning was issued though.

'Lydia, when we get back home we will stand on the balcony together and we will throw away all the distractions of this summer,' said Valery, looking over at Lydia's wrist with her right eyebrow slightly raised.

Lydia could honestly not understand how adults could be loving and obnoxious at the same time, in the same moment. She decided to enjoy her bracelet, may the end of the summer bring whatever it had to.

As promised, on their return to Ploiesti Valery and Lydia stood on the small balcony of their apartment and said goodbye to all the little shiny accessories bought over the summer. For a split second, Lydia thought that she might be able to convince Grandma to go outside and play so that she could find them and sneak them back inside but then she remembered the incident with the mittens full of coins and how that ended. Best to do as Grandma had planned.

Lydia felt loved, looked after and nurtured so she was willing to pay any price because she wanted to belong.

Every now and then, Grandma Val took Lydia to visit Sergiu's parents, Mr and Mrs Munteanu in Bucharest.

Beginnings

Her father's parents were professional artists, or so Valery described them to Lydia. Her grandfather Tudor was a photographer, and her grandmother Maria was a fine brush painter. She was several years older than him and that seemed to mean something to Grandma Val, although Lydia didn't understand what.

They had three children, two boys and a girl, all in their late thirties. Her father's older brother George had a son around Lydia's age, named Val (short for Valentin), who her grandma told her to play with when they visited.

To be honest Lydia couldn't care less about Val – he always wanted to play with his cars which she found boring. And Val found little interest in Lydia because she didn't share his passion for vehicles, so the sentiment was mutual. But they pretended to play together, most of the times in an adjacent room, so that the adults could talk.

Lydia didn't like visiting that house nor the people in it. The whole building smelled old and foul. Maria rarely smiled, and she would always receive them in bed, as though she was ill. Tudor was always grumpy and not very entertaining, he spent their visits walking in and out of the living room which made Lydia feel very uncomfortable. At the end of their visits, she always felt a sense of relief to be out of that building, breathing the air in the street. It was a polluted air, as you would expect in any capital city, and yet, to Lydia, it felt welcoming and liberating. She felt no connection with them, at all.

But Grandma Val said that it was important to go and see them twice a year, so they did.

⁓

Lydia looked at her empty cup and the corners of her mouth formed into a gentle, nostalgic, smile. She stood up and walked over to the coffee machine, preparing for another delicious drink. Her motions were trance-like. She kept thinking about how perceptive children are. Little Lydia knew, back then, that no good can come from places with fouls smells. And yet, she told herself that children are taught to disregard their intuition and apply the knowledge of their parents, or, in her case, grandparents, when it comes to social conventions.

On one occasion, when Lydia was around eight years old, Grandma Maria sat in the bed, propped up against and amongst her cushions, and she studied Lydia from behind an old pair of spectacles, with her thin lips pursed shut and her white hair carefully brushed. After a long moment of silence and staring, she finally spoke.

'Do you know, Lydia, I always wondered if you were truly my son's daughter, but now that you are growing older, I am beginning to see the resemblance.'

Lydia looked at her, puzzled. Grandma Val sitting next to her started to say something but was abruptly and, in Lydia's opinion rudely, interrupted by Maria.

'Well, you know, dear, you are an unwanted child after all, since your mother was not married to my son when she fell pregnant with you. He had to marry her …' There was an unpleasant silence, loaded with meaning, the interpretation of which escaped Lydia at that moment.

Valery, on the other hand, fully understood Maria's comments and felt that it was time to end these visits. She stood up sharply, grabbed their coats and stormed out of that horrible place with Lydia following close behind.

Beginnings

'You are my darling, smart, beautiful and beloved granddaughter and Granddad George, and Uncle Marvin, and your cousins, and I love you very, very much, that's for sure.'

Lydia had never seen her grandma so angry, and she felt her heart going out to her, in love and gratitude.

This is how Lydia found out about her beginnings and the word 'unwanted' would haunt her for many years to come. Considering that she had been told how babies are delivered by the stork to their parents' doorstep, the words uttered by Maria filled Lydia with confusion and fear. Yet it made sense that she was unwanted, given that her parents didn't live with her and instead her grandparents were in charge of her upbringing. Lydia sensed the cruelty of the revelation and at the same time, she was, in a sense, grateful to Maria, for shining some sort of light onto the mystery of her circumstances.

When they arrived back home, Lydia was sent to the bedroom because Valery wanted to discuss their visit to the Munteanu's with George. After they talked, Grandma called Lydia and announced with relief in her voice that they would not go back to that house nor see her father's parents for as long as Lydia was under their care. Lydia never felt more satisfied with any of her grandma's decisions as she did in that particular moment.

When the summer of 1976 ended, Lydia received the news which would change her life forever.

She was told that her mother and father were finally able to receive her. That they had made huge effort, especially her mother, to obtain a travel visa from Romania to

Lydia's Journey

western Germany and that at last she would be reunited with them.

Her grandparents seemed very happy with this news, and she was told how lucky she was that her mother had managed to petition a popular politician, who had approved or had had some influence in Lydia being reunited with her parents and her brother.

Lydia's heart skipped a beat. She was perfectly happy where she was. Grandma Val and Granddad George were her parents. She was loved by the people she knew. She had friends. She was getting good grades and was top of her class. Why then, was she being punished and sent away? Could somebody please make sense of all this?

School started and everybody knew about her news. She felt so sad. She had to leave behind everyone she had known and loved for so long. She had no idea where she was going. Nobody could tell her what it would be like. She didn't even remember her mother, what she looked like, what she was like, not to mention her father who was rarely to be seen in the pictures. He left the country when Lydia was three years old and even when he was still living there, in Bucharest, he never, not even once, came to visit her at her grandparents' house. Instead he met with her during the summer, for a couple of days or so.

She was sent to be reunited with strangers! For her, this was not a celebration. This felt like a death sentence.

Lydia felt terrified. Lost. Unloved. Unwanted. Cast away. Adrift. Uprooted. Unheard. Unseen. Insignificant to the people she loved.

She forgot her superpower.

Beginnings

Her grandparents decided that she should learn German, so they hired a tutor. Lydia was supposed to go to her apartment, a couple of buildings away, for one hour every week. She started skipping her lessons and wandering around the block with friends, in the hope that she would make her grandparents understand that she did not want to leave them to go to Germany. Of course it didn't work, yet they were not willing to pay if Lydia wouldn't attend the lessons, so the German learning stopped.

That year Christmas was quieter than usual. The same celebrations, family meals and festive dinners were prepared but a sense of sadness lingered.

Lydia was expecting Santa, hoping for a miracle of some sort, maybe he could make this nightmare go away.

Two days before Christmas, Lydia was playing with her old dolls in the bedroom while her grandad was in the living room doing crossword puzzles from the newspaper. Lydia was dressing and undressing her dolls and talking to them when she noticed that one of them was missing a hat. She looked around but it wasn't in the little suitcase where she kept her dolls and their accessories. She wondered if she had dropped it when she took it out of the wardrobe. She opened the wardrobe door and started looking for it, moving her grandma's bags and boxes, searching for that hat. All of a sudden she noticed a box, standing at the far end of the cupboard. The most beautiful doll she had ever seen, tall, blonde, was looking at her with glass blue eyes. She was so beautiful and Lydia could barely contain her excitement. She ran out of the bedroom, straight into the kitchen where Valery was making dinner. She stood there, waiting to catch her breath.

Lydia's Journey

'Grandma, Grandma, you will not believe it! Come and see! You will not believe it!'

Valery looked at her, 'What is it? Calm down, Lydia, what is it?'

'Come on, come on! You have to come and see it! It's the most beautiful doll I have ever seen!' Lydia was beside herself with joy.

Grandma had no choice but to follow Lydia into the bedroom and stand in front of the wardrobe as Lydia opened it again.

'There, look below, there she is! Isn't she beautiful?'

Valery bent down and looked where Lydia's little hand was pointing.

'I see nothing, sweetheart,' said Valery. 'There is no doll. Are you sure you didn't just imagine it?'

Lydia did not believe her. She bent down to look herself. It was like an ugly trick, the doll had disappeared. She looked up, to her grandma, then looked back again into the wardrobe but the doll was not to be seen. She even started to move the bags and boxes around, but it had gone.

'But ... it was there, I saw it, it was there ...' Lydia's voice began to break.

'Let's go back into the kitchen, sweetheart, I've made pasta,' said Valery, after she gave her a kiss on the forehead and a gentle stroke on her head.

Lydia felt stupid, again. She doubted herself, then was angry, then gave up because she could not prove what she had seen.

Beginnings

Two days later, on Christmas morning, Lydia woke up and went to look under the tree where a wrapped box, about the size of what she had seen in the wardrobe, was waiting with her name on it. It was the doll. The joy was still there, mixed with some reflective thoughts: *What if Santa is not real? What if her grandparents buy the gifts, wrap them up and then put them under the tree?* Finally, the anticipation of unwrapping her gift took over and Lydia put those doubts and questions in the back of her head.

Several days later, when Lydia asked her grandma about that night, Valery told her the truth. When Lydia ran into the kitchen, George, who had listened to the conversation between Lydia and Valery moved the doll to a high shelf and buried it under piles of folded shirts to keep up with the Santa illusion, thus Lydia could no longer find it.

The magic of Christmas was beginning to fade away, but Lydia decided that no matter what she had been told about Santa, in her heart, he would always be there for her.

Her departure was approaching quickly, and for Lydia this day signalled the end of everything she knew, jumping without a net, being thrown into the water without knowing how to swim – something that did actually happen, one of her father's brilliant ideas one summer while on holiday with her grandparents by the lake.

The night before her flight, Lydia could barely sleep. She was so anxious. She kept tossing and turning in the bed while her grandparents were in the living room watching television. And that's when it started.

Lydia's Journey

On the night of the 4th of March 1977, around 9.20 p.m., there was a weird sound, like the wind blowing through tall trees but louder, then a slight tremor started to shake the building. It rapidly increased in intensity and it felt as though the entire building was bending and twisting, creaking sounds came from the walls, furniture slid about, dishes shattered on the kitchen floor and books dropped from the shelves. Lydia's grandparents rushed into the bedroom to get her – she was already by the edge of the bed, trembling. They grabbed her and stood under the door frame in the hallway, waiting for the tremor to pass. They heard shouting in the hallways, people running downstairs and out of the building, screaming at each other, knocking on doors on their way out to wake up their neighbours and save as many as possible. Granddad George stood firm and didn't move, it was not safe to run outside while the building was still moving, and everybody was crowding the stairs. So, they stayed put. Holding each other tight, they waited for the earthquake to pass.

Later that night, the news said that it was a 7.5 magnitude earthquake. It shook the earth where Lydia lived and killed many people.

Once the tremors stopped, Valery held Lydia by her hand, and together with George went downstairs and walked out of the apartment building, gathering with the others in the alley. Lydia remembered that everywhere she looked, people were scared and talking and pointing at the buildings surrounding them.

It was late at night, but nobody seemed to want to go inside. And it was bitter, winter chills still lingered in the air. Lydia was only wearing her pyjamas and slippers when they left the apartment. Finally, she tugged at

Beginnings

Valery's hand telling her that she was getting cold, and although she didn't feel safe going back in, she was getting *really cold*, and she was hungry.

They headed back to the apartment but none of them were tired or wanted to go to bed. Valery made sandwiches and they sat at the dining table eating in silence.

Lydia thought that she could still feel the floor shaking under her feet.

When they finally decided to climb into bed, it was about 1 a.m. Lydia was sleepy, and was ready now to turn in for the night.

One hour later there was an aftershock which measured 4.9 on the richter scale, but Lydia was so exhausted that she didn't care about being dragged out of bed and carried in her grandma's arms to the hallway door frame. They stood there, waiting for it to pass, and Lydia only remembered that her grandma carried her back to bed and sleep finally came. But it didn't last long because Lydia had a plane to catch at 7 a.m the next morning.

She was woken up way before dawn and rushed into her clothes. After a quick breakfast, Uncle Marvin was ready to drive them to the airport.

The journey was about an hour and a half. When they arrived at the outskirts of Bucharest, Marvin had to drive very carefully through the ruins of a city in mourning.

What Lydia saw that morning, through the car window as they drove past, filled her with fear and sadness, with a sense of helplessness and a question which had no answer. Why?

Lydia's Journey

Collapsed buildings, wires poked out from broken walls, pipes leaked, dogs sniffed amongst the ruins and howled once in a while. The day grew lighter, the mist lifted, and Lydia started seeing more people searching in the rubble, some were crying, others sat in silence. It was a desolate picture of a ruined city and Lydia could not help but think how much the outside world matched her inner one, her own world, crumbled and in ruins, the life she knew gone. She felt like one of those people who sat and cried for their lost loved ones, but unlike them she was not understood. Lydia's sadness and despair were not acknowledged. She was to leave all her loved ones behind and be 'reunited' with her parents and brother.

When they arrived at the airport, shards of broken glass covered the floor and they had to navigate their footsteps carefully.

Lydia had a small suitcase – she didn't have many clothes and her grandma said that it would be better to have nice, new clothing bought by her parents, as a welcome gift so to speak.

The moment to say goodbye came. Lydia dragged her feet over to Valery, not wanting to hug her but feeling that if she didn't, she would never forgive herself. Valery kneeled on the hard floor and opened her arms widely. Lydia tucked her face into her grandma's coat and opened up her senses to absorb as much as she could and treasure it in her memory. She was afraid she would not see Valery again. Then she heard Grandma's voice whispering in her ear.

'I love you Lydia, be brave and make me proud.'

Grandad put a hand on her shoulder and Lydia had to let go of Valery. She hugged them all, one by one, holding

Beginnings

back her tears, wanting to appear brave, then followed the security guard who was in charge of delivering her to the plane – like a piece of luggage, from here to there.

Lydia wanted this nightmare to be over quickly, and she rushed behind the security guard, not wanting to look back. She was too scared to cry and yet her whole being was screaming with rage inside. Against all training and teachings, she felt a wild beast awakening inside her in that moment, filled with emotions she didn't know existed. She wanted to scream and punch and kick and shout and cry her eyes out at the insanity of this moment.

When they arrived at the plane, she climbed the stairs attached to the outside of the cabin and was handed over to a flight attendant who would watch over her during the three-hour flight.

The moment she walked onto that plane, Lydia knew that this was not a nightmare, this was real, and she had to find a way to deal with it.

Chin up, man up, shoulders square and no tears. This is a big person's world and this nine-year-old girl had to prove to her new set of adults that she was an asset of some sort so they would keep her with them.

She didn't remember what her mother looked like, nor her father. And she had never met her little brother, Liviu

Those were the people with whom she was about to be reunited. They were her family from now on.

The plane started to move, and soon she felt it take off.

Lydia had three hours to decide on her strategy with her new family. She felt alone. She was alone. Sat in her seat, in the big cabin, full of unknown people, flying high above the clouds, leaving behind everything she ever knew, moving towards an unfamiliar destination. She had to find a way to ensure nobody would ever want to send her away again. She had to make sure that everyone from now on would like or, even better, love her.

Lydia felt like this was the biggest promise she ever made to herself. And the biggest cage she would put herself in, without knowing what was about to unfold and the price she would have to pay in order to fulfil her promise.

Chapter 2

'When life becomes a dirt path of obstacles and thorns, the only way to change it is by living one day at a time.'

Lydia, 2022

The plane was shaking and hurtling through the air, making an incredibly loud noise inside the cabin. From where she was sitting, Lydia could hear the engines roar and sometimes a draft blew into her face.

This seemed pretty much like a trip through hell, and she started to feel a headache developing around her temples.

Somehow it helped to pay attention to the outside conditions rather than the overwhelming world of her emotions. She was flying to a destination on a map, to be reunited with people from photographs she had been shown since she was four years old. She was about to meet and live with her parents who had left her behind, in the care of her grandparents, more than five years ago.

Lydia's Journey

The people she thought loved her and would be there for her sent her away. The people she was about to meet had no connection to her heart. She regarded them as strangers.

Better to pay attention to what was going on in that cabin than to let herself be engulfed by the fear of the unknown ahead of her.

Finally, the pilot announced something through the loudspeakers, impossible to understand with all the noise that was going on, and she felt the aircraft start to descend. She saw the flight attendants go back to their seats and strap themselves in and she realised they would be landing shortly.

Through the windows of the aircraft, she saw fields and some roads as they quickly approached their destination. Finally, the wheels touched the ground and the plane soon came to a halt. Everybody in the cabin clapped. What for? Lydia didn't know.

Then, they all stood up, got their suitcases and bags, and checked for their belongings. Lydia carried only her small suitcase and she started to march in line towards the exit. When her turn came to step outside, she looked at the flight attendant who had kept an eye on her during the flight and understood that this was yet another goodbye.

She walked down the stairs and was received by a man, dressed in a flashy, fluorescent vest who said something in what Lydia assumed to be German – now she started to regret not following up with her lessons – and pointed towards the cart he was driving. He lifted her up and helped her take a seat. When she looked around, Lydia was surprised to see two other children, a similar age

Beginnings

to her, sitting in the cart on top of suitcases, just like her. When she tried to talk to them, they looked at her and answered in a different language. Lydia could not understand them, so she sat there, her arms around her suitcase resting in her lap, and waited.

The cart started to roll through the airport and Lydia felt lost – literally – she had no idea where she was being taken or what to expect. It stopped for the other children to be picked up – by their parents, Lydia assumed – and she found herself alone, riding through the airport in a luggage cart.

They finally stopped again, and she had to turn around to see what the driver was doing. As she turned, she saw a woman dressed in a cream-coloured, three-quarter length winter coat, waving at her and smiling. Lydia turned her head, thinking that the lady was waving to somebody behind her but when she couldn't see anyone waving back, she turned again, and saw the woman was walking towards the cart with her arms open and a big smile on her face.

'She must be my mother,' thought Lydia and tried her hardest to form a smile with her lips.

'There you are, my precious. Finally! I have missed you so much,' and her mother gave Lydia a big hug and helped her onto the ground.

The cart pulled away and Harriet bent down, looked at Lydia then gave her another hug which made Lydia sneeze because her mother's coat had a fur neck, very ticklish in her nostrils.

'Come on, my dear, you must be hungry and tired. Let's get you out of here,' and they started walking through the airport. Harriet held Lydia's hand. Lydia did not like the contact of that hand, but she was indeed tired and hungry, therefore she overlooked her first impression.

They left the ground floor of the airport and walked upstairs where they entered a room with tall glass walls and several chairs lined up against them. Lydia noticed a man, standing with his hands behind his back, facing the windows. When her mother greeted him and called him by his name – Sergiu – Lydia knew that this man was her father.

Sergiu turned around and looked at her. Lydia felt small and intimidated but she had made a promise to herself, so she approached Sergiu and stood in front of him looking up. Sergiu patted her on her head and mustered some sort of a 'welcome' and then the three of them left the airport heading towards the car park.

They got into the car, her mother sat next to her in the back seat and handed over a sandwich.

The journey home lasted over two hours and Harriet kept talking to her and asking her questions. Lydia was so exhausted from the emotions and the long flight, yet she tried to keep up with her mother's enthusiasm even though her headache seemed to get worse.

Finally they parked outside the family home and Lydia got out of the car and followed her parents inside.

When they entered the house, they were greeted by Uncle Kosta, her mother's older brother, and Liviu. Uncle Kosta, who was also Lydia's godfather, picked her up and held her tightly against his cheek. Although Lydia was tired and confused and suffering with a splitting headache, she felt the same warmth and love that she did in the presence

Beginnings

of Uncle Marvin and her grandparents. And for a brief moment, Lydia didn't feel that lonely and lost.

But the moment passed, and Lydia was put down where she had to face and meet her little brother who stood in front of her, a questioning look in his eyes and a toy car extended in his hand towards her. He wanted to play with her and his cars.

Fortunately her mother said something along the lines of, 'Lydia is tired, my love, so let's all have dinner and then go to bed.' It was truly late, past Lydia's bedtime anyway, so they all had a quick meal, after which Uncle Kosta left and the four of them got ready for bed.

'Lydia dear,' said her mother, 'why don't you hop up into bed with us tonight, I'll give you some painkillers for your headache and you can sleep and rest until the morning? Would you like that?'

Lydia didn't really know what she wanted, other than to rest in a safe place, and she couldn't refuse her mother's offer, so she nodded.

Harriet prepared a bath for her, helped her to get into it and play a little, then helped her out. When she was ready for bed, she went and said goodnight to her father, then followed her mother into their bedroom.

Harriet wanted her to sleep in the middle of the bed, so she crawled under the covers and fell asleep. It was a restless sleep – new bed, new sheets, new place, new people. Dreams popped in and out of her head. She tossed and turned all night long. In one of her dreams, she felt like a hand was touching her, head to toe, but she was so drained from all the events past that she couldn't make out for sure what that was and when the morning came she forgot all about it.

Lydia's Journey

The next day was a Sunday and when she woke in the morning the house smelled like toasted bread and coffee, yummy! Lydia got out of bed and went into the kitchen. The door was open, and her mother was busy preparing breakfast for them. The door to the dining room was also open, and she saw the table, set with a nice tablecloth and dishes.

Her father was sitting on the sofa reading something and her brother came up to her from his bedroom, looking at her again with that curious gaze.

'Good morning,' said Lydia with a soft voice and her mother turned around, gave her a big smile and a hug, and then handed her the bread basket.

'Could you put that on the table, my dear, and then come back,' and Lydia did as she was told.

This isn't so bad, thought Lydia and when she finished helping her mother with the breakfast, they all sat down and ate.

Her parents lived in a two-bedroom ground floor flat in a three-storey building. In the flat above them was a family with two young girls, close to Lydia's age, and above them two elderly sisters.

The town seemed quiet, and Lydia wondered if her parents went to church, like her grandparents did?

A couple of weeks later, it became clear to Lydia that Jesus was not a part of her new family's lives, and she did not mention anything about him to them. It was to remain her secret superpower and she was happy to keep it that way.

Her knowledge of the German language was close to zero and her mother was not happy about that. One day Harriet decided to send Lydia to the bakery, on her own,

Beginnings

and buy bread for the family's breakfast that morning.

Lydia was terrified. It had been only a few days since her arrival! Surely her mother would accompany her, but she was mistaken. Harriet wanted Lydia to learn the language and this seemed the best way to do it, since Lydia had proven to be uncooperative when she had had the opportunity to have German lessons – that's what her mother told her to justify the request.

Lydia took the money and listened carefully to her mother who spelled out what she had to say, 'Zehn taffel brötchen, bitte,' meaning, 'ten bread rolls, please.'

All the way to the bakery, which was probably a ten-minute walk from the house, Lydia kept repeating to herself, 'Zehn taffel brötchen, bitte, zehn taffel brötchen, bitte …' but when her turn at the counter came, she forgot half of it. Fortunately, the lady serving her seemed to have a kind soul and asked Lydia to point out what she wanted, and, in the end, Lydia came back home with the errand done.

Lydia understood after this how important it was to learn the language.

It was in the beginning of April 1977 when Lydia started school. Her parents had arranged for her to attend one nearby and she started only three weeks after her arrival in Germany, not speaking the language, not understanding a word. She sat in her chair and listened to the classmates around her, to the teacher, without being able to speak. She was not inclined to regret past errors of judgement and yet, the lack of perspective she had proven by dismissing the lessons provided by her tutor in Romania was hurting her deeply now.

Lydia's Journey

One day when she went to get her coat from the rack outside the classroom, she was ambushed by three of her classmates who felt offended that Lydia did not speak German. It was not the first time that Lydia had been punched by a fellow pupil. When she was in the second year in Romania, a well-placed fist to her solar plexus from a boy in her class had knocked her to the ground and she had lost consciousness. She remembered waking up in the arms of Miss Ana. Her teacher sat her on the edge of a big table in the staff room, brought her a glass of water and stood with her until she was sure that Lydia had fully recovered. That incident caused some commotion in school, it was very rare and the boy was severely punished in his behavioural grade.

This time, Lydia was quick enough to turn her back to them and protect her body and face as much as she could. They pushed her against the coats and started pounding their fists into her head and back, saying some words which Lydia translated later into a hate speech against foreigners who don't even bother to speak German and yet are allowed to go to a German school.

When she came back home that day, she didn't want to tell anybody about what had happened, but her mother saw her face and noticed Lydia was hurt. She talked to Lydia's father about it, and he took his daughter aside.

'You will have to toughen up and start fighting back if you want them, and others like them, to leave you alone. You will have to prove yourself worthy of respect and become stronger. You will have to learn how to defend yourself. Tomorrow you will come along to my school.'

Sergiu was the owner of a martial art school in town and the next day Lydia began her training in how to defend herself from bullies.

Beginnings

Her mother reported the incident to the headmaster and for a while the boys kept their distance from Lydia.

Lydia attended her father's dojo class twice weekly. Dojo was a series of different combat techniques, a blend of many martial arts combined into what Sergiu wanted to develop as a single, integrated model, his model. Lydia learned how to keep her equilibrium, focus her attention inwards, kick and punch, roll without hurting and throw her adversaries over her hip or shoulder. She learned how to perform a kata and was trained in combat.

Lydia became proficient and enjoyed herself in this new exercise and role. Her confidence grew and she felt grateful for the opportunity to learn how to keep herself safe. She started to change her first impression of her father and began to feel that she might like living with her parents after all.

She was eager to please and her father did seem satisfied with her progress.

In the meantime, her mother was teaching her German and Lydia participated more in class. Although the bullying didn't completely stop, it became bearable, and Lydia kept improving her martial art skills and her German language proficiency.

Her mother insisted that she slept in her parents' bedroom, although almost two months had passed since her arrival. One night, as she was about to fall asleep, she began to notice what she had thought of as a dream: a hand going up and down her body. She froze, afraid to breathe or move. She knew it was her father's hand. Lydia

Lydia's Journey

was trapped. Her mother was snoring, her back towards Lydia, and she could not move. The hand stopped after a while and Lydia fell in and out of sleep all night. She was afraid and did not know what to do.

Early the next morning, the family had a trip to the countryside planned, Sergiu loved fishing. They packed the car and hit the road. Sergiu was driving and because Lydia suffered with motion sickness she sat in the front seat, next to him. The trip took them out of town and into the country, two hours away from home.

Lydia didn't say much that morning, not knowing what to do about what had happened during the night. One thing was certain though: it had not been a dream.

'Lydia, dear, you're awfully quiet,' said her mother from the back seat, 'are you feeling alright?'

'Yes, Mum, I am alright,' muttered Lydia, although she did not sound convincing so her mother prodded further.

'Did you sleep well last night? When you woke up this morning you looked as though you had seen a ghost.'

For a moment, Lydia dared to hope that maybe, if she told her mother what had occurred during the night, it would not happen again. She took a deep breath.

'Last night I felt a hand moving across my body and I was scared to fall asleep.' Her heart started beating faster and Lydia felt that something was not quite right around her. A heavy silence filled the air and she realised that it might have been a mistake to open her mouth and let the words out.

'Oh, sweetheart, it was a nightmare for sure, not worth paying attention to it,' answered her mother and they all fell silent.

Beginnings

And there it was: the confirmation of her mistake. In that moment, Lydia felt alone, terrifyingly alone, and although she did not understand then what frightened her that night, it was now clear that her mother would not be there for her, she would not pay attention to what Lydia had to say.

They arrived at the river and got out of the car. Sergiu decided upon their spot for the day and then asked Lydia to walk with him and get some firewood while her mother and brother started unpacking the car.

Lydia followed her father and for a while nothing seemed unusual. But once they turned a corner behind tall bushes and were beyond sight and out of earshot, Sergiu turned around, came towards Lydia, and pushed her shoulders so she fell back into an area of the riverbank heavily populated with nettles. Lydia had to put her hands behind her back to soften the fall and that's when it started to sting. Her hands, arms, even her cheeks, were covered in a myriad of tiny blisters from the contact of the nettles with her young skin.

'Nobody will believe that nonsense you were talking about in the car. You should know that I do not tolerate liars in my house. If you carry on like this, I will be forced to call the police and they will come and take you and lock you away, for that's what they do with little liars like you. Because that is what you are. A shameless, insignificant little liar.'

As Sergiu towered over Lydia she started to cry, and she rubbed her eyes which instantly began to sting.

After giving her a fierce look, Sergiu turned around and started walking away.

Words fell short in describing how Lydia felt in that

moment. She had been raised to be resilient and resourceful, to rely on her inner strength and to chin up, man up and square off her shoulders in the face of a challenge. She had also been taught to rely on the adults in charge of her upbringing, to trust them and respect them, to love them and care for them. At the age of nine, Lydia yet again met with her destiny and had to make a quick decision: persist in telling the truth to the adults around her now who clearly did not believe in what she had to say, who threatened her with the police, or, to shut up and deal with it on her own way, the best she could. And because of the promise she had made to herself on that plane, she got up, determined to make it work anyway, and followed her father along the riverbank. The problem was that Lydia did not know what 'dealing with it' meant. She could not think of a way to keep safe while pleasing everybody around her.

From that moment on her childhood, as she knew it, was gone. Her nightmare, on the other hand, was about to begin.

One good thing did happen after that trip. Her mother sent her to her brother's bedroom to sleep, where she would have a bed by the window, and from that day on she and Liviu shared a room.

The school year was almost finished and one morning Lydia's mother told her that the headmaster had invited them both to his office for a chat.

They attended the meeting where he advised Harriet to transfer Lydia to a special school for foreign children who did not speak German, where she would be enrolled in a programme to help her learn the language.

Beginnings

Harriet looked at him, then she looked at Lydia and then back at the headmaster.

'I do appreciate your concerns about my daughter and your advice in terms of her academic options. However, I do believe that my daughter's educational needs are best met in your school therefore, with all due respect, Lydia will stay where she is.'

'I'm afraid your daughter is not fluent enough to progress adequately in her studies,' added the headmaster, obviously frustrated at Harriet's decision not to transfer Lydia to another school.

Her mother stood up and extended her hand to the headmaster.

'Lydia is a bright child, she will be fluent in German by autumn,' and she ushered Lydia out of his office.

Despite Lydia's opinion of her mother, in that moment Lydia admired her confidence in her daughter's ability to learn and decided to make sure that she would not be disappointed.

It was agreed with the headmaster to allow Lydia to enrol in the school year below in order for her to catch up with the curriculum. And this is how Lydia ended up a year below her classmates. For Lydia, being held back by one year did not seem to be important.

That summer, Lydia followed a strict daily programme of four hours of German lessons imparted by her mother and twice weekly self-defence training sessions at her father's martial arts school.

Sleeping in her brother's bedroom had put a stop to the

Lydia's Journey

hand and Lydia felt a massive relief about that and her confidence and self-esteem started to develop. She began smiling again and felt more like herself.

She and her mother would go shopping together and Harriet would buy her nice clothes. But Lydia was not allowed to wear any type of trinkets, not even in the summer, because her father once sat her down and told her that, 'jewellery on a woman's body let's everyone know how much she is worth.' Lydia looked at him wide eyed and felt cheap because she could not stop herself from wanting to wear bracelets and rings and necklaces, even though she would not be able to do so for many years.

The holidays ended and it was time for Lydia to start the school year. It had been an intensive summer and she felt ready for the challenges ahead.

It was a short walk from her house to the schoolyard and Harriet and Lydia made the journey together that morning.

The classroom was big, and the windows were tall and wide, the tables were nicely arranged for the students and Lydia, followed by her mother, picked one of them then sat down looking around. She felt satisfied with her choice. Unlike the two-seater desks lined up in rows in her classroom in Romania, here in her new school the tables were square, allowing four pupils to sit around them and they were placed lining the walls so that they all had access to the centre, and they all had a clear view of the blackboard.

Miss Gertrude Mohler, her teacher, seemed friendly and she introduced the year's curriculum to all the parents

Beginnings

and children present at their first meeting.

Lydia was now officially enrolled in her first full year in a German school. She felt excited about it, although a little scared of the expectations of her. Yet she felt ready to prove herself in a foreign school system.

Lydia's natural character soon prevailed, and her cheerful personality helped her to make friends and enjoy school again. To everyone's surprise, although not to her, Lydia started getting high grades in her homework, just as she used to in Romania. She made her mother proud, and her father seemed to be pleased with her progress through the coloured level system in his dojo.

Christmas was only two months away. It would be Lydia's first Christmas with her parents, and she wanted to learn how to play some festive songs on her parent's electrical organ. Harriet had been trying to teach Lydia, but Lydia seemed to want to learn her own way – which Harriet never understood. Since Lydia had proven to be determined in achieving her goals, they set her a challenge: Sergiu placed a bet that Lydia would not be able to play five Christmas songs by Christmas Eve.

The race against time was on and Lydia added organ. practice to her daily routine.

Her brother, Liviu, was a creative three-year-old, he made cars by carefully cutting boxes (toothpaste boxes were his favourite), using wheels from real toy cars, then placing little Lego people in holes he created for the passengers. He would spend hours rolling them back and forth on his bedroom floor. He also made a game out of calling out Lydia's name, with no purpose whatsoever, and when Lydia rushed to him Liviu would just look at her and then go back to his cars or, after a while, he would just ignore her.

Lydia's Journey

When Lydia had enough of that nonsense, she told her mother about it. Harriet would say, 'He's only three, Lydia, you as his older sister should show more understanding and patience towards him.' No point in complaining, Lydia told herself, so she stopped.

But when Liviu began to understand that he had allies in his imaginary race to become the favourite child, he stepped up his tactics. He made it into a game to climb into Lydia's bed early in the morning before she woke, put his chin against the top of her head and then push down hard. The first time this happened, Lydia awoke with a jolt, finding her brother on top of her shoulders, pinning her down. It hurt, badly, and in her daze from being woken up like that, she tried to release herself from his grip using her body and strength. She looked at him, furious and shocked to read in his eyes the pleasure he took from this action. Of course, Lydia told her mother about what just had happened, yet Harriet reacted as expected.

'Come on, Lydia! To come up with such stories at your age, it's ridiculous, darling. Please stop making things up.'

Lydia felt helpless. Whatever she did or said regarding her brother's mischief, was not tolerated. Lydia felt as though she constantly took the blame.

Well, if that's the case, then Lydia had to take matters into her own hands. And she did. Nearly every morning her brother woke up before her and climbed on top of her shoulders, and Lydia learned that if she pinched him hard he would release his grip and leave her alone. But events had taught Liviu that his mother would take his side, so one day as Harriet put a coat over his shoulders he flinched and pulled away as she touched his arm.

Beginnings

'Liviu dearest, what's wrong? Are you hurting?' she asked him.

Liviu, with a coy smile on his face and a sad bowed head, stood there without saying a word. Lydia, who witnessed the scene, felt trapped, again.

Harriet moved closer to him and uncovered his arm, where she could see some small bruises.

'How did this happen? Liviu, I want you to tell me how this happened!' her voice full of anger.

Her brother kept silent, but he turned his head slowly, towards Lydia, and gave her a look which said, 'I will always be her favourite!'

And that was all that her mother needed to know.

Harriet waited for her husband to come home that evening to tell him about the incident and show him the bruises on their son's arm. Judging by his attitude, Lydia started to fear what was about to happen.

'I will need to take some time to think,' said Sergiu. 'You need some stronger discipline. Lying about your brother doing things to you is one thing, but hurting him and leaving marks on his body, that changes everything. Your mother and I have been patient with you so far. You have been raised by your grandparents and I have to admit that some of your habits – lying, inventing things – need to change. We will talk about this tomorrow.' He went and sat on his favourite place on the sofa to watch his favourite television show. Harriet got up from her chair. Liviu, who had been on his mother's lap during his father's speech, was looking at Lydia and smirking.

Lydia could never forget that smile of victory on Liviu's face. And to her, it was the most infuriating aspect of

Lydia's Journey

this entire incident. Her brother had found a way to manipulate her into taking the blame for his abuse. Lydia could not believe that she had been tricked into this. That night, when she finally stopped her heart from pounding, she sat on the edge of her bed and though about how the entire event had unfolded. She had to admit that she had been outsmarted by a three-year-old child. She also acknowledged that there was nothing akin to love or safety about this place or the people who were in charge of her now. She felt terribly lonely that night, and for every night she continued to live under the same roof as her parents. She cried herself to sleep, curled up under her blanket and she felt the overwhelming weight of injustice holding her down, against her will and against that bed.

The next morning came and Lydia sat down at the dining table and ate her breakfast in silence. Everyone was sombre that morning except Liviu, he was just being himself.

While she finished her meal her father went around the sofa, with a long, thick piece of rope in his hand. He placed it down in a circle on the carpet, then asked Lydia if she had finished. Lydia nodded so he motioned for her to come to him, which she did.

'Now, Lydia, this is the circle of your shame,' he announced in a solemn voice. 'You will get in there and crouch on your hands and knees until you understand what a terrible thing you have done and you ask for forgiveness from your brother, your mother and me.'

Lydia went into the circle, bent down on her knees, then onto all fours. She looked at the carpet: it was brown. The rest of her family stood there for a while, then left her

Beginnings

alone as they went on about their business. Liviu bent over her, trying to make eye contact. Lydia had enough of him and his vicious mind. She ignored him, on purpose, which went against her core training, but she had to. She felt humiliated. Deeply humiliated. And she was in no mood for watching the smile on his face. For all she cared, in that moment, he could go to hell.

She spent what seemed to be an eternity in that position. Her shoulders ached, she couldn't feel her arms any longer and she started to fidget, losing the pose. Her back seemed to arch downwards and the bottom of it started to feel very heavy. She did not know exactly how long she spent there.

Finally Sergiu came to her and asked, 'Are you ready to apologise for what you have done?'

'Yes.'

At last Lydia was allowed to stand up. She felt a bit dizzy but that passed quickly.

She said sorry to her brother. He smiled at her with deep satisfaction in his eyes. She then apologised to her parents. They stood in front of her, towering and majestic in their adult power, and patted her on her shoulder after she promised not to lie or invent things about her brother, ever again. Box ticked. Harriet said something about the value of honesty between the family members and Sergiu just turned his back on Lydia and walked into the kitchen. The incident appeared to be forgotten. Only Lydia could not forget. Over the years spent in her parents' household, she might have fooled herself about forgiveness, but one thing was certain that day: she could not forget the circle of her shame. But she did make sure that she was more careful in choosing her actions and words from that day on. Those people in charge of her upbringing were not to be trusted. They had different standards which did not resonate with Lydia's heart, yet she would not break. But she would have to bend and twist herself into a pretzel if she wanted to please them.

Her days became routine – school, dojo, home, weekends and back to school again. She was happy at school and soon Lydia made a close friend, Erika.

Christmas break came upon them, and Lydia was excited to see how her parents would celebrate the season.

Her mother decorated the house and the day before Christmas Eve, she asked Lydia to keep Liviu entertained so that she could put up the Christmas tree without the boy intruding. Harriet would then tell Liviu afterwards that Santa had left the tree.

'Oh, I know,' said Lydia to her mother, 'it's what Grandma used to do, send me out with Granddad on Christmas Eve.' So this year Lydia, as the older sister, was in charge of keeping Liviu away from the living room. Luckily, her mother locked the door shut. Obviously she knew little Liviu better than Lydia. He escaped Lydia's watch a couple of times, running down the hallway and trying to open the door. But finding it locked he had to turn around and find some other entertainment.

Finally Harriet was ready and she announced in a triumphant tone that Santa had been and left the tree so that he would know where to visit the following evening.

It was a magnificent tree. Lydia went close to smell the scent and she could not believe how beautiful it was. Full of branches, thick in needles, tall, up to the ceiling. The ornaments shone in the candlelight and Lydia was

Beginnings

ecstatic. Her face glowed with excitement, and she hugged her mother tight and thanked her.

The next evening, although Lydia was well aware that Santa did not exist she could not avoid getting caught up in the magic of Christmas Eve and Santa's visit.

At around 6 p.m. the doorbell rang and Harriet went to open the front door.

Liviu and Lydia followed her into the hall and there he was: Santa Claus in all his glory!

Full costume, beard, hat, gloves and bell. Lydia could not believe her eyes. It was like walking into a dream. It had been so long since she last had seen Santa. At her grandparents' house, before they moved into the apartment, Santa would visit every Christmas, with a bag full of gifts, wrapped in shiny paper. He would knock on the front door and Grandma would invite him in. Then he would ask for the children of the house to come forth and Maribel, John and Lydia would line up in front of Santa and recite poems in exchange for their gifts.

Lydia's eyes started to fill with tears at those fond memories and she had to pull herself out of them and come back to the present moment: standing with her brother and mother in the hallway of the building, receiving Santa in the year 1977.

Santa was carrying a big red bag, full of wrapped boxes.

Harriet invited him into the house, and he went and sat down on a chair she had already prepared for him. She had placed a glass of water and some cookies by the seat, just in case Santa was hungry or thirsty after such a long

Lydia's Journey

ride from the North Pole. Then Liviu and Lydia took turns in receiving their gifts which Santa pulled out of his bag and handed over to them in exchange for their songs or poems. He was a skilled Santa, Lydia thought, he would have had her fooled if she didn't know all about him already. Yet she didn't mind. She looked at her little brother and saw his eyes sparkling with joy.

That night was a particular triumph for Lydia, because she exchanged her five organ Christmas songs for her gifts. She felt very proud at this achievement because she had taught herself those songs. She won the bet and her father had to pay her the money owed, after he was done playing Santa.

The shower of presents and laughter filled Lydia's heart with the magic of Christmas. She had never seen as many gifts in one Christmas, never ever. She opened boxes, put wrapping paper away then opened yet more boxes. In one of them, she found this funny, apple-shaped piggy bank, with an opening in what seemed to be a quarter slice cut away. When Lydia turned the metal key on one side, a worm came out of the opening, grabbed the coin and pulled it back, until it fell with a clunk into the apple. She had never seen such a clever design and loved how realistic this gift looked.

After Santa finally left, they had to wait for Sergiu to 'come home from work' to tell him all about their special visitor.

When he finally returned, the family sat at a beautifully decorated Christmas table and ate delicious food prepared by her mother.

The next morning, Uncle Kosta came over and they told

Beginnings

him all about Santa's visit. Kosta had a gentle smile on his face which reminded Lydia of her granddad.

That Christmas would remain in Lydia's memory as the most magical she had ever had.

Then the winter break was over – Lydia went back to school and her daily routine. Lydia liked routine, it made her feel safe and in control of her circumstances.

Over the school year Lydia excelled in her studies. She started to score highly in school and the day that the headmaster had told her mother it would be best to transfer Lydia to a different school was forgotten.

That year, Lydia came second in her class, and she felt really proud of herself. So was her mother.

Before long the summer holiday was upon them, and a surprise was about to be revealed. Her parents decided to go on a road trip that year and at the beginning of the summer of 1979, Harriet, Sergiu, Lydia and Liviu embarked on a journey that took them through France, Belgium, the Netherlands and Denmark and its islands. Lydia would have had the trip of her life had she not had to sleep on top of an improvised bed over the trunk of a minivan, sharing the space with her little brother who tossed and turned all night long, every night, in his sleep. Yet it was an adventure. Her father stopped at riverbanks where he set up camp and went fishing. They bought food in the villages along the road, and it felt to Lydia as though they were travellers. The weather was mostly nice but, in some pictures Harriet, Lydia and Liviu did not look very happy. Years later, when Lydia enquired about those photographs, her mother reminded her that she had suffered from terrible sciatica due to the sleeping arrangements and that Sergiu had refused to shorten the trip because of that so they had argued and spent the second half of their journey angry at each other.

How interesting that when we focus on one particular thing, it can limit our perception and understanding of the whole.

Lydia remembered the day they spent at the famous Tivoli Gardens, the countryside they had visited, the endless fields of tulips in the Netherlands and the windmills rising tall to meet the North Sea winds. She was amazed at how tall the Eiffel Tower was and she enjoyed the ferry ride they took to move between the mainland and one of Denmark's many islands.

The road trip lasted over three weeks and Lydia felt exhausted when the minivan finally pulled up in front of their house.

Lydia spent the rest of that summer playing outside, in the gardens belonging to the property. Sometimes her upstairs neighbour's older daughter would play with her, but they didn't like each other very much.

One day, Harriet took Lydia shopping into town where she saw a Barbie doll unlike any other she had seen before. This one had a caramel latte skin and she looked smart thought Lydia.

Lydia pleaded with her mother – she really wanted that doll – but her mother wasn't easily persuaded. Then Lydia remembered, when she was small and living with her grandparents, how her mother had once told her that

Beginnings

she could not have everything she wanted, nor everything her friends had.

Lydia wanted the doll badly. Harriet looked at her and then finally said, 'I tell you what, Lydia, let's wait and see if you still want that doll in a couple of months, and if you do, then I will reconsider.'

Lydia could not wait that long. When they arrived home that day, she went into the bedroom, picked up her piggy bank and began counting the coins. A big smile broadened across her face when she realised that she had enough money to buy the doll. She kept that information to herself and waited.

She needed to plan her actions carefully this time. One day when her mother left the house to go shopping Lydia snuck outside, jumped over the terrace wall alongside her parents' bedroom and went into town by herself. She walked into the shop and picked the Barbie up, tugged the box against her chest and felt like the happiest ten-year-old in the world. She went to the checkout, paid the cashier, put the doll in the plastic bag and then rushed home before her mother came back.

A short while later Harriet arrived home. She placed the groceries on the kitchen counter and when she turned to open the fridge, she almost bumped into Lydia who was standing by the kitchen door, holding her hands behind her back and smiling at her.

'Lydia dear, what is going on?' asked her mother.

Lydia wanted to wait a bit longer, but she could not resist the joy and pride in herself that she felt in this moment. She turned her back to Harriet for a split second so that she could rearrange the box in her hands and then turned

Lydia's Journey

around, holding the treasure in front of her mother, accompanied by the biggest grin Harriet would ever see on her daughter's face.

Her mother was surprised. Indeed, she was. She put down the item she was holding and came closer to Lydia, looking at the box.

'What have you got here, Lydia, is that the doll you showed me at the shop the other day?' Harriet could not believe it.

Lydia told her the story, about how she had climbed up the terrace wall and gone to town, how she had paid with her own money and how she had made it back home.

Lydia was so happy that her mother could not say or do anything to deny her that doll. It was bought with her own money, after all. Lydia realised that, unlike Grandma, Harriet was not going to scorn or punish her for using her savings to buy something, even if the item was for herself.

'I wish I knew you wanted that doll so much,' was all Harriet could say. This confused Lydia, since she had made it very clear, or at least she thought she had, that she really, really wanted that doll. It didn't matter anyway; she was holding the prize in her hands.

Her mother agreed to buy some clothes for the doll in exchange for Lydia promising that from now on, she would let her know when she intended to buy something and her mother would take her to the shops.

Harriet was concerned that Lydia would make climbing walls and sneaking out of the house a habit, so she wanted to make sure she knew what her daughter was planning in advance.

Beginnings

That day Lydia felt like a conqueror. She felt more mature and she was thrilled at the courage she had proven to herself. Lydia was growing up.

As summer ended, Lydia and Erika sat together again, ate lunch together and spent most of their time in school with each other. They became even closer friends than before.

One day Erika invited Lydia to her house to play and after getting permission from her parents, the girls spent a wonderful afternoon.

The following week Lydia was invited again and she went, with her parents' approval.

A week later Lydia came home and asked her mother if she could have Erika over to their house to play. 'No!' said her father.

'This house is off limits for any friends. Now and forever,' said Sergiu. And he meant it because her parents never entertained. They never had friends over. In fact, as Lydia soon began to realise, her parents didn't have any friends.

No friend ever came over to Lydia's house. Not Erika, not anybody, for as long as Lydia lived there.

After a while, Erika stopped asking Lydia over. They still played together in school but that was about it and their friendship cooled. Lydia did not understand her father's reasoning so could not make Erika understand it either.

One day in October, Lydia's parents announced that Valery and George planned to come and visit them. Lydia nearly jumped out of her seat with joy at the news.

Lydia's Journey

She was so thrilled at the prospect of having Grandma and Granddad with her again. They were due to arrive sometime the following February.

Christmas time brought joy and gifts. Santa visited again, although this time he only brought a couple of presents for each child, he listened to their songs and poems, and then left. The tree was beautiful although not as stunning as the one the previous year. Lydia had lots of fun with the new Christmas rituals at her parents'. When her father 'came home from work', he stood there at the front door.

'Has Santa been already? He seems to have left something out here, on the front steps, guys! And it has your names on it!'

Lydia and Liviu came running out to take a look.

Two beautiful race cars, one silver and red, and a smaller one that was black and yellow. Name tags assigned the yellow and black to Liviu and the other to Lydia. They looked amazing! Liviu was giggling and running back and forth between his mother, his father and the car. Lydia felt just as happy as her little brother and could not believe how beautiful and comfortable the car seat looked and felt. It was covered in red faux leather and was padded. What luxury! She loved it.

The next day, it didn't matter to either child that it was freezing and heavy snow had covered the entire town overnight. They took their cars out to the garden and started racing them up and down the alley until their noses became cold and red and they realised how hungry they were.

Another fun and eventful Christmas had passed, and Lydia was now looking forward to the arrival of her grandparents.

Beginnings

The night before their arrival in early February 1979, Lydia could barely control her excitement. Over the period of time that she had been living with her parents, Lydia had learned not to give away her thoughts and feelings too easily. She was afraid that if her parents, or even Liviu, realised how happy she was about Grandma and Granddad visiting, then something terrible might happen to prevent them from doing so. And it seemed ironic to her that she had been induced into this deceitful behaviour by the very people who had accused her of the same, when she learned to keep her thoughts, emotions and actions to herself while crouched on all fours inside the circle of her shame.

The happiness in her heart was too big though to be overshadowed by such thoughts and Lydia decided to focus on her inner joy and wait for the day to arrive.

And now the day had arrived! That morning, way before dawn, she jumped out of bed and went into the kitchen to help her mother, who was already busy preparing breakfast before their car ride. Once they had finished, her mother laid the table for the arrival of her parents and they all put on their heavy coats and went out to the car. They all got in and her father turned the key. The car didn't make a noise. He tried again, with the same result: nothing.

Oh no! thought Lydia. *This is not possible! It can't be! How are we supposed to go and pick up Grandma and Granddad without the car?* She felt like crying in frustration.

But her parents, after cursing their luck, called a taxi to come and drive them to the airport. They had to ask Uncle Kosta to stay and watch Liviu since there would not be enough room in the car for all of them to travel to the airport. They arrived just in time to see Harriet's parents walk out of the customs area with their suitcases and a big smile on their faces.

Lydia couldn't stand it any longer! She broke free from her mother's side and dashed through the foyer, running towards her grandparents. She hugged them, and they kissed her and told her how much they had missed her, and she felt like she was home again, she sensed their love and felt that she was safe. She was not one to look back nor give into regrets, but at that moment, basking in their affection, she realised just how much she had missed them.

Her parents approached, and after hugs and welcome wishes, they all turned to the exit and left the airport.

Back home Uncle Kosta was waiting and Valery and George got to meet their grandson Liviu. It was such a joyful moment for Lydia. Her uncle joined in and her brother, as usual, was curious about these new people. They finally began to relax, unpack and talk, talk, talk. Lydia just sat there, next to her grandmother, watching her parents and her grandparents, watching her uncle Kosta and seeing how happy he was to be seeing and chatting to them again, having left his home country so many years before. Everybody was talking, food was served by her mother, drinks were poured into their glasses by her father and uncle Kosta, and Lydia fell asleep that night grateful for the gift she had received: her grandparents here, with her, all three together again.

The month her grandparents spent in Germany was the month Lydia felt the most alive in a long time. She went to places with them and her parents, she spoke to them endlessly, she showed them where she went to school, she told them about how she was learning martial arts and she wanted to know everything about the loved ones

Beginnings

back home in Romania. Maribel and John, Uncle Marvin and her friends from school, Miss Ana and everyone she could think of. Because to Lydia, her home, the one place she felt loved and safe was at her grandparents' apartment. She might have left them behind when she had boarded that plane, but she had never left her home, the only home she would ever know.

They took trips to the countryside, went to cities Lydia had never been to before, visited museums and cathedrals and Uncle's Kosta new home.

Lydia did not want this visit to end. She did not want her grandparents to leave. But the day had come when they had to say goodbye.

Lydia stood at the departure gates, crying and waving as she watched Valery and George disappear into the crowd. When they got back to the apartment she was met with silence and a sense of emptiness. She felt the lack of life and laughter, and that night she cried herself to sleep once more.

The days went by without enthusiasm, or joy, or any goals. Lydia did not want to live without her grandparents, and she started to eat less, laugh less, communicate less with the people in her life. She went to bed every night and fell asleep crying, her pillow wet with tears the next morning. Her mother questioned the reason for her sadness and Lydia, who did not want to enter the circle of her shame again, confessed that she was upset but refused to expand on the reason why. Lydia had lost her spark and Harriet started to become concerned. She discussed her worries with Sergiu who said nothing about it. For the time being.

School had always been Lydia's pride and joy and during

this period it became the only place where Lydia wanted to be. She returned to her books and assignments and although she was still gloomy and quiet, she concentrated on her schoolwork and her dojo training to ease the hurt in her heart.

Springtime with new flower buds, and the buzzing of the bees, and the scent of the flowers in their neighbours' gardens, finally came. The sunshine started to melt the ice on the ground and began to warm up Lydia's heart once more. She understood the inevitability of her circumstances and little by little came to terms with them. Her grandmother wrote to her more often than before, probably because Harriet had said something Lydia thought, and she treasured these letters, keeping them safe in her bedside table.

That year Lydia finally got to see the benefit of all her efforts in martial arts. It was during a PE class. The pupils were split into teams to play hockey matches in the big gym hall. Lydia was in the middle of a game when Tom, one of her classmates, came over and started accusing her of losing the ball on purpose or because she was stupid. He was quite intimidating and, without any word of warning, he slammed his hockey stick against Lydia's right ankle. The teacher didn't see, he was on the other side of the hall watching the others play, and the only potential witnesses to this incident were the classmates sitting in the gallery waiting for their turn on the floor. Lydia was furious and her ankle hurt badly. He had smashed his stick straight into the bone. Their game was coming to an end and their teams were asked to move to the benches in the gallery and wait. As they walked towards their seats, Lydia looked over to Tom who was

Beginnings

laughing with his friend Hans, and looking over to her. In that instant Lydia knew that she would become the laughing stock of the entire school if she allowed the incident to pass without doing anything about it. But what could she do? The teacher hadn't seen what had happened and she was not willing to ask her classmates if they had witnessed anything. That was too tedious and to Lydia it seemed pointless.

She walked up to Tom and tapped him gently on his right shoulder. He turned around to Lydia standing in front of him and looked at her with an enraged expression in his eyes. Lydia could not understand what could have triggered such a reaction, surely not the missed shot?

'What do you want?' asked Tom, 'Go away, you useless …' But Lydia didn't wait for him to finish. She had had enough of his attitude and malice.

'I want to pay you back for what you did to me,' she said, emboldened. She could see the surprise in Tom's eyes and a vicious smile starting to curl down the corners of his mouth.

They were standing in between the benches, without much room to move.

Tom squared his shoulders and looked into her eyes.

'You've got some nerve, you brat. Maybe I should tell you that you are standing in front of a green belt in judo.'

Lydia moved fast, in her brain and in her body. She understood that a judo competitor would not know how to block a punch so she threw one into his face, aiming for the left-hand side of his jaw. Her fist was tight, and her aim was clean. Tom's face moved towards his right shoulder with a jolt, and he lost not just his balance in

Lydia's Journey

that moment, he also lost the confrontation. He did not know that Lydia was a green belt herself in her father's dojo. She had been participating in competitions for over a year. Lydia stood there; fists ready for a second launch but it was not required. Tom – under the wide-eyed gaze of their little audience, including Hans – turned his back on Lydia and walked away, defeated.

After that incident, which did not have any consequences other than a short meeting between her parents and her teacher, nobody dared harass Lydia for as long as she attended that school.

It would not be the last time that Lydia had to assert her ground with physical force and every time it happened, her reaction afterwards would be the same: uncontrollable sobs, shaking her body. She did not ask for violence, she did not want to hurt, yet sometimes it was required. Lydia felt ashamed of having to use force in order for her voice and wishes to be heard and respected. It was a cruel world when she was growing up and, unfortunately, it still is.

During Easter 1979, Lydia's mother took the children to visit Uncle Kosta at his new home, a village about a three-hour drive away. He had bought a bar and Harriet wanted to help get the place ready for opening.

Kosta had graduated as an agricultural engineer. After World War II he had worked in Romania on a farm and married one of the younger students at university, Gloria. Harriet loved telling the story about her brother and sister-in-law escaping the country by train. Apparently, Uncle Kosta and Auntie Gloria had decided to flee the Communist regime, as they were both university

Beginnings

graduates and in those days it was dangerous to be highly skilled. They had a plan: to board the train crossing the Hungarian border and to hide in the toilets during passport checks at customs. But they had not taken into account that every corner of that train would be inspected. As they were approaching customs and the train was starting to slow down, both Kosta and Gloria stood up from their seats and walked over to the toilets in between the long, second-class coaches. But, there was a problem: the ticket inspector was blocking their way. Kosta, walking ahead of Gloria, asked for permission to pass through. As expected, he was asked to present his train ticket and passport. Uncle Kosta pulled out both and handed them over. Cool and calm, so the story went. The inspector looked at the passport then enquired about Kosta's travel visa, as he saw none. As Kosta started to mumble, losing confidence in his plan, Gloria made her move: she stepped in front of Kosta and with a shrieking sound fell into his arms pretending to have fainted. Kosta held her and requested to be led to the toilets straight away. The inspector looked puzzled, then scared, as he did not know how to handle an unconscious passenger, and he finally moved aside, to show Kosta and his fainting wife to the toilets. He gave the passport and train ticket back as he was opening the coach door. Pretending to revive his wife, Kosta asked Gloria for further instruction, both squeezing into the tiny toilet of the slowly-moving train. They kept splashing water around, then they realised the train seemed to have gained speed again – during the commotion they had crossed the border. They had to leave the toilet and just go with the flow. A new ticket inspector was approaching from the other end of the train. Kosta looked at his wife, then at the inspector and when asked to show his passport and ticket, Kosta calmly replied: 'I have already been checked by your colleague.' This was a bold move. Raising his eyebrows, this new official looked at Kosta, assessed his calm demeanour and then decided to make eye contact with the inspector at the end of the coach from where Kosta and Gloria had come. The exchange was fast: eyebrows raised, thumbs up and ... the miracle had happened. The ticket inspector led them to their seats and left. It sounded like a story from a novel rather than real life, but Harriet believed it to be true and Lydia went along with it. There were some puzzling questions which Lydia wanted to ask, but on second thought she decide not to. Her mother then told the story of their failed marriage – after spending several months in different refugee camps across Europe, once Kosta and Gloria arrived in Germany their marriage hadn't worked out and the couple finally decided to put an end to their ordeal and get a divorce.

This happened several years before Lydia went to Germany and since then her uncle had tried out different jobs with little success. Finally, he seemed to have settled upon becoming a bar owner, and when an opportunity came along he took it without hesitation.

He had an old building, with the bar on the ground floor and the living quarters above it. The rooms were generous and bright, with a faint, musky smell. The living room door opened onto a terrace at the back of the building and overlooked the dusty patio of the property.

Harriet and the children spent about a month at Kosta's, redecorating the place and making it look pretty. It was exciting to play outside on the back patio with their racing cars and their uncle loved having them around.

Shortly after the opening of his bar, Kosta and his new

Beginnings

fiancée, Martha, announced their wedding date. Harriet started visiting more often, at weekends, and they got to meet Martha and her family and friends. She seemed nice. Her parents too. Lydia and her family were invited to her uncle's in-laws-to-be for a weekend.

The wedding day came and Lydia, as the ring bearer, had a special place in the carriage which waited outside the churchyard to take the newlyweds from the church to the bar, where the wedding party would take place. It was a charming ride, Lydia thought, and she enjoyed it very much. Uncle Kosta was definitely a romantic, Lydia concluded. The couple seemed very happy.

It was the first wedding Lydia remembered and she enjoyed it. The following day Harriet and Lydia stayed behind to clean the place up before they drove back home. Sergiu and Liviu had left earlier, they did not need to clean up anyone's mess, so her father said.

The abundance of good news during the year of 1979 did not stop there. It turned out to be a great year for Lydia as she soon found out that her parents had decided to move back to Romania that autumn.

Could it be true? Lydia's eyes opened wide, her heart started to race with excitement and happiness at the prospect of seeing her grandparents again.

It was true! Her parents decided to make the move back in stages. First, her mother, brother and Lydia would make an initial trip to Romania – Lydia was not given the reasons, nor did she care about them. All she wanted was to be back home again. Lydia wished for school to end,

Lydia's Journey

and she wanted it to end now. Eventually the school year did come to a close.

The first weekend of the summer break they packed some belongings for the trip, said goodbye to Sergiu and headed for the road.

Harriet drove for endless kilometres, stopping and resting, eating and sleeping, until they finally arrived at the Hungarian–Romanian border.

Lydia had never seen a more breathtaking landscape as she had witnessed during this three-day car journey with her mother and brother. The beauty of nature was awe-inspiring. And the prospect of the joy of being reunited with her loved ones in Romania just enhanced the spectacle.

Once they crossed the border, the ride to Ploiesti seemed to happen in a dream. They only spent a couple of weeks there, she was told by her mother that this was a trip to re-familiarise themselves with the city. Romania's government was opening its borders slightly, encouraging citizens living abroad to return. Although Lydia now had to brace herself for the long journey back to Germany, her mother, her grandma and every adult she asked confirmed to her that her parents were serious about moving back to Ploiesti, close to Harriet's parents. Lydia just had to be patient and wait for this dream to become a reality.

They drove back to Germany and finished packing, selling and closing down their businesses. Her father had to close or sell the martial arts and music schools, Lydia didn't know which. Her mother had to stop tutoring her private music students.

The night before her father and brother left Germany,

Beginnings

the family ate their dinner at a camping table and said goodbye. Sergiu wanted to start their journey during the night, apparently due to traffic. He and Liviu, who was half asleep, left that night and Lydia and her mother would tidy up and get ready to leave shortly after.

Lydia did not know why her parents had decided to leave separately. When her father phoned Harriet from Ploiesti, three days later, confirming that he and Liviu had arrived safely, Harriet set the day of their departure.

Lydia and her mother would also leave their home in Germany at night, in a minivan packed with items to be used for selling or bribery once they had arrived at their destination. Wow! Bribery, that was a new concept to Lydia who sat in the front, with a mini television unit squeezed between herself and Harriet, barely able to stretch her legs. When she looked behind she could hardly see the rear window, the space was completely packed. Lydia had a sense that they were running away that night, rather than simply returning to Romania. She could not shake this feeling – the overloaded vehicle and her mother asking her not to make too much noise on the way out of the house, as to not wake the neighbours. There was something strange about their departure, but Lydia concentrated on the trip ahead, on helping her mother to follow the road map and on the end destination – home.

Something about watching through the car window at night while her mother drove through towns and on motorways added to the magic of this journey. Lydia felt exhilarated. She could remember how devastated she felt when she made her first voyage on the plane from Romania to Germany, and now that she was finally going back to her homeland she could barely control her excitement. Happiness overflowed her senses. She was

Lydia's Journey

too young to understand why her parents had decided to move back to their home country, and although she comprehended some of the basic rules and guidelines of the government in Romania, she lacked the maturity to assess her family's reasons behind their decision to return to Romania.

Future years would bring some clarity on the subject, but Lydia never questioned the motives. She only knew that, for once, her parent's reasons and her own wishes had coincided and that was all she cared about.

They drove during the night and rested during the day. Her mother was an experienced driver and Lydia only felt scared once, when they had to stop and sleep at a petrol station during their second night on the road. They locked the van and spent a couple of hours in the uncomfortable seats until her mother felt refreshed enough to continue.

They were in the former Yugoslavia and got lost in the mayhem of Belgrade's roads, but after a few turns and redirections, they again found the sign pointing to the way out of the city.

They reached the border with Romania around midnight on their third day of travel, and they had to wait in a queue of cars before they actually reached the check point.

When the officer came to inspect the papers and the vehicle, Harriet started to act nervous, and Lydia sensed that something might be wrong with their paperwork. As it turned out, it wasn't the documentation that was in question, it was the merchandise that was at risk of being confiscated. As they waited for the officers to decide how to proceed, Lydia made out some familiar figures on the other side of the barrier which separated the two

Beginnings

countries. They were quite a distance away but Lydia could clearly see Uncle Marvin, her father and Granddad, waving at them and making reassuring signs. Her mother saw them too and when the officers came back to the van with a decision, Harriet started talking to them and pointed towards her family waiting on the other side of the border. The officers asked Harriet to start unloading the minivan so that they could perform a thorough check of it and Lydia thought that her mother might lose her patience with them. However, there was no arguing with a border officer. The entire contents was unloaded onto benches, a task which seemed to take forever. The van was thoroughly searched, dogs were brought in, nothing suspicious was found, and they were allowed to reload it and move on. The entire operation cost her mother a few pairs of brand new jeans and some other items from their haul. So bribery was a real thing, Lydia thought, and it seemed to have worked.

By the time they left customs and crossed the border, it was early afternoon. They had spent nearly fourteen hours at that station and Lydia felt a huge relief when the car finally started to roll through the gates and touched Romanian soil.

Her mother parked nearby, following Uncle Marvin's car and when they finally got out and hugged each other, Lydia felt that the nightmare was over.

If only she knew which way the path was going …

Chapter 3

'Perhaps it is the "not knowing" what awaits us which allows the human spirit to shine brightest in the darkest of circumstances.'

Lydia, 2021

When Lydia woke up she forgot where she was for a moment. She looked around the room and sat there, at the edge of the mattress on the floor, hoping to force the memory back into her brain.

And then, she remembered. She was in Ploiesti, her birth town, living in a studio with her mother, father and brother.

It was the beginning of autumn 1979 and Lydia was eleven years and nine months old. This was a temporary situation, her parents told them. Thank goodness for that. It was so small, and it felt more like a trap than a studio.

The building itself was a ten-storey block of cement with no aesthetic or architectural style whatsoever. It was like

Beginnings

a rectangular matchbox. It was located in the south of the city, close to the train station and alongside a beautiful boulevard lined with tall, old chestnut trees. A place to promenade on Sunday afternoons and meet with friends or family; somewhere one could sit outside, on a terrace, while sipping a cold pint of lager or a lemonade. A blend of busy and relaxed which Lydia loved to watch.

Since their arrival, a couple of weeks earlier, life had been hectic for her parents. They had so much to deal with – between organising jobs, housing, school and nursery the days were going by fast.

There was also something which began to worry Lydia. The hand had started to come back. They all slept on a king-size mattress on the floor. She did her best to stay away, she was the last going to bed so that she could lay at the edge, next to her mother and it didn't matter to her that sometimes she would wake up on the cold linoleum floor, having rolled out during her sleep. But the hand seemed to find her more often than not. And Lydia knew that she could not talk about it with anybody. She felt terrified at the memory of the nettles, her father towering over her and the threat of him calling the police. But she also felt scared that she would not be taken seriously by her grandmother if she dared pour her heart out to her. Lydia knew it was real and it revolted her, yet when she imagined the scene of her telling Grandma about it, she was met with Valery's stern face and a questioning look. And one thing Lydia couldn't bear was disappointing Grandma Val. Lydia was sure that Grandma would feel let down by Lydia making things up, as her mother would put it.

Lydia's Journey

So Lydia never told Valery, nor George, nor anyone she loved, about her nights and the hand. Somehow, she felt that by not telling them, they would be spared the shame of the police knocking at their door.

School had already started, and Lydia had been registered at the same school that Uncle Marvin taught mathematics. She would have to take the bus there and back each day.

It felt weird to Lydia to go back into a classroom with two-seater desks lined up in rows to fit as many as thirty-five pupils per class, and at first she struggled to fit into the rigid school structure with an overwhelming curriculum. However, it also felt familiar, and Lydia soon fell into old habits of learning.

She made friends and one day a girl called Clara invited her back to her home. Lydia was undecided – she wasn't sure it was a good idea, but she did enjoy playing with Clara so she went. She didn't tell her mother or anyone else about it. Several hours passed before Harriet finally found out where she was and came to pick her up.

'I wish you would have told me about you visiting Clara today. I was worried sick. If it happens again, I'll have your father pick you up, Lydia, do you understand?' her mother wasn't shouting, but Lydia understood the meaning of her words.

For a while, Lydia remembered not to visit without asking permission first. Until one day she forgot. And that day, her father came to pick her up from Clara's house.

Sergiu took Lydia to Uncle Marvin's where Harriet was babysitting Maribel and John and Liviu was playing with them.

Beginnings

When Lydia entered the apartment, her mother gave her a look which said, 'I told you what would happen …' and her father took her straight to the children's bedroom.

The quieter he was, the more Lydia realised that whatever punishment he had planned, it wasn't going to be quick.

She perched on Maribel's bed and waited. She was scared but did her best not to show it. Her father pulled over a chair and sat down. He gave her a long look.

'Lydia, you don't seem to understand the rules of our family. I thought I made myself clear when you spent time in that circle of your shame, that I would not tolerate disobedience.'

He paused for what seemed to be an eternity and Lydia thought that maybe he was waiting for her to say something.

'I'm sorry, I didn't mean to. It was a mistake,' she said, not sure that it would change anything.

It didn't.

'Well, your mother told me that this is not the first time. I have to say, I'm not pleased to hear that she covered for you. Maybe if she hadn't, you wouldn't have to face the consequences today. But she did, and you will,' he said standing up and putting the chair back where it belonged.

He then asked Lydia to lay face down on the bed.

Lydia started shaking. She did as she was told. From the corner of her left eye she saw her father holding a long, thick, dark red walking stick. The lights went off.

Lydia relied on her ears now, she listened to the footsteps approach and then stop by her bedside. And then silence, until the air moved and she heard a swishing sound – and felt the blow.

The stick made contact with her bottom and Lydia could not suppress her scream. In the past, when punished, she did not yell or plea. She cried, in silence.

But this blow and the following, were nothing compared to what had come previously. Each time, the pain would feel like an explosion inside her brain and body, an inner scream which left her drained. Her senses were heightened in the darkness, she waited for the stick to make contact, knowing it was about to happen from the sound it made through the air. Lydia's attention was focused on pain and fear: high levels of anticipative fear.

She lay in the darkness, pressing her face against the pillows, and refused to cry or scream again. After several blows were met with utter silence, she heard her father's voice from above.

'Why don't you cry? Why don't you cry?' he repeated, seemingly irritated by her stubborn silence. That was the moment when Lydia understood that she had the upper ground in this violent display of brute force. And this made it easier to receive every single hit afterwards, knowing that her father realised that he could not make her cry at his will, nor through violence.

Finally, her father was exhausted and stopped. He asked Lydia to get up and turn on the lights. She did as she was told. But when she attempted to obey, she realised how painful it was to move her muscles from the waist down. She walked with difficulty, her bottom felt as hot as a baking oven and every movement was agonising.

She could not sit for several days afterwards, and she was afraid to look in the mirror because of the big, dark bruise.

Beginnings

Nobody said anything about this disciplinary method. She was prohibited from visiting her grandparents for a while, and they never knew what had happened nor the reason for her absence. They were told that she was being punished for disobedience. And they never questioned it. After all, parents are supposed to teach their offspring the rules of the world.

Time can play tricks on bruises. Lydia did not know whether the ones she carried would heal or scar.

After a couple of months of living in the studio, the family moved into a bigger place, a two-bedroom apartment in a new build, a ten-minute walk from Lydia's grandparents. The landing of the building had four apartment doors, two on each side of the staircase, and it had the same layout on each floor. You had to climb four steps on the landing to reach their apartment door, the first on the left if you entered from the back or the second door on the right if you entered the building from the front.

Lydia walked into the apartment behind her parents, following them down a long hallway which led from the entrance to the living room. The first door on the left opened to a long, train-wagon like bedroom, which her parents decided would be the children's. Next came the kitchen, wide enough room to fit a small four-seater table and chairs. The table could lean against the wall when it wasn't used for meals.

A spacious living room marked the end of the hallway. The entire apartment was south-facing and the light shining through the wide windows made it look pretty. There was a door on the far wall of the living room which lead to a small square hallway, holding a pantry on the right-hand side, a bathroom straight ahead and on the left the main bedroom where Harriet and Sergiu would sleep.

They moved in at the end of October and this would be Lydia's home for the next eight years.

The bedroom assigned to the children was very narrow, it wouldn't fit two single beds in it so their parents decided to buy two extendable armchairs to be placed back-to-back and kept extended. This is where Lydia and Liviu would sleep. Their 'beds' would be laid against the left wall. A desk placed against the right wall by the window, a wooden storage unit for books and schoolbags and a tall two-door wardrobe was all the furniture that bedroom could accommodate.

The living room was fitted with a wall-to-wall, floor-to-ceiling chestnut cupboard, which held most of their clothes. On the left-hand side was an impressive bookcase and television unit, just as tall and large as the cupboard, and opposite that was a three-seater sofa flanked by two armchairs in the soft colours of the living room. A coffee table in between the seating area and at the far end of the sofa an upright piano would complete the layout of the family room.

The master bedroom had a double bed with one side table on Harriet's side, and placed on the other side of the bed and close to the window was Valery's extendable desk where Lydia used to sit and do her homework in her grandparents' apartment before she left for Germany.

Once the apartment was furnished, it looked more like a home.

After they moved into the new place, Lydia also was enrolled in a new school. German lessons were on the

Beginnings

curriculum and Harriet made clear that she expected her daughter to excel. A different school also meant that Lydia had to say goodbye to Clara.

This new school was known for its high academic standards and Grandma Val seemed very content that Lydia would be going there. Harriet had to 'donate' some jeans, but Lydia's place was secured.

Lydia started shortly before Christmas and fully integrated back into the Romanian education system. She continued to be a good student and achieved good grades. Now she was older the academic demands were higher. She discovered that she did not like algebra, yet she enjoyed geometry. History was a drag, but she liked the teacher, he seemed a nice, quiet person. Literature and grammar were her strengths and passion. She also enjoyed biology and, later on, anatomy while chemistry puzzled her. In art and crafts, she managed to sew herself a nightshirt – it was two sizes too big, but she persevered. Her music teacher seemed to think of Lydia as her favourite – much to Lydia's annoyance – because Sergiu and Harriet were both professional musicians.

Lydia did not know how to read musical notes, however she had an excellent ear and a great memory so she pretended to read, yet simply imitated the notes her teacher had given the class at the beginning of the lesson. She performed superbly and her teacher never realised, although Lydia did not like the feeling of deception. One more black mark in her dishonest attitude towards the adults around her.

Sometimes her grades were low but there was no direct punishment, and she thought this might have been because her brother did not share her passion for knowledge therefore his school performance was pretty poor. Occasionally her mother would be called to school to discuss strategies to improve Liviu's attitude towards learning and his grades. Lydia could relax a little knowing that she would not suffer big consequences for bringing home a lower mark once in a while. Her competitive spirit was in part the motivation for her academic performance, yet she learned because she wanted to know, because she was curious to find out about the world around her. It became obvious that she was skilled in the human sciences, so it was only logical for her parents, especially her mother, to assume that she would pursue a medical career in the future.

Unlike during her primary school years, Lydia decided that learning for herself was more rewarding than studying simply to achieve high grades. This line of thought signalled a change in her final results. She was no longer first in her class, but she was in the top three pupils every year.

She did have to use violence once more, a couple of months after she started her new school, but that was the last time she would have to do so. One of the known bullies in her class, a girl as tall as Lydia but apparently stronger, judging by her muscle mass, challenged Lydia's patience by repeatedly ruining her homework. Lydia was generally patient and would seek the silver lining in situations, but no one was going to touch her elaborate homework and walk away from it. One day, snow covered the school grounds and some of her classmates went outside for a short break while Lydia, and several others stayed behind in the classroom. This girl, who appeared intent on causing distress, came back inside and smashed

Beginnings

a snowball against Lydia's open homework book. The ink started to run instantly and, like the bull can't stand the colour red, Lydia could not bear to see the running ink of the elaborate handwriting she had spent hours working on. She stood up from her seat and looked the perpetrator straight in the eye. There was malice glaring back at her. Malice and a question: 'What are you going to do about it?' Then, those eyes turned away and her classmate started walking down the aisle. Lydia followed and, with a sense of déjà vu, tapped her on the right shoulder and before any exchange of words could happen, Lydia jumped at the girls uniform, twisted her and held her bent over, by the back of her head, arm wrapped around what Lydia thought it was her throat. Others gathered around and shouted, they soon made Lydia aware that she had to let go as her classmate was falling limply at her feet, lip split and blood flowing. Lydia felt terrible about inflicting violence on another human being. She left the scene, went outside the classroom, stood against the wall by the door and started crying softly. This was not what Lydia had intended. She stood there until her teacher found her, sobbing against the wall. She had to explain what she had done to her teacher, to her parents and to the mother of the other girl whose lip remained swollen and bruised for several days. Harriet had to talk to the headmaster and Lydia had to promise never to do it again. As though she was in the habit of displaying such behaviour. This was not how Lydia wanted to leave a mark and make an entrance. She wanted to be acknowledged and remembered for her academic achievements, not for her aptitude in self-defence. In time, with perseverance and dedication to what she loved most – books and knowledge – she would be able to transform her reputation as a potential bully into one of an ambitious student and she was remembered for her grades in exams and her end-of-year results.

Lydia's Journey

Not long after they had moved into the new apartment, Lydia's father began to develop some sort of depression. He stayed at home for days on end. He sat by the living-room window, sometimes rocking back and forth, without saying a word. Just staring at the walls. This scared Lydia as she was not able to understand what it was, she felt uneasy and sometimes threatened by the presence of her father on that armchair in the living room.

Once she started sharing a bedroom with Liviu the visits from Sergiu at night were scarce. But as he grew more confident that his son slept soundly they had become more and more insistent. She had no place to hide, nowhere to run. She was trapped, especially when Harriet had to step in and take a job she disliked, as an administrator and event organiser at the history museum in town. Lydia and Liviu came home from school and did their homework, Liviu in their bedroom and Lydia in her parents' room, where the old, black desk was waiting for her, every afternoon, just as her father was.

She did her homework and would then escape, in her head, to her fantasy world, the only place to be, the only way to keep going, until her father allowed her to leave the bedroom.

Lydia was twelve years old when her father started to pay her regular visits. And she was twenty-four when she finally broke free. But in those early days, she only knew one thing: she had nowhere to turn for help.

One night, after she returned from her safe place in her head, just before she was about to fall asleep, she felt a familiar feeling in her heart, and she remembered her superpower: she remembered how safe and loved she had felt in that big house called church. She remembered her own discovery about Jesus and from that moment, Lydia

Beginnings

never felt alone in her heart again. She had to deal with life in her own way – unsupported, unacknowledged, unheard, unseen – yet, she did not feel alone nor forgotten. So that night, after the pain had subsided, with the love of a deep connection to something bigger than anything around her, Lydia fell asleep with a gentle smile on her lips. As strange as it may have sounded, Lydia found safety and reassurance in the power of a love beyond this world.

The next day Lydia told her mother that she would like to start accompanying Grandma to church. Valery could not have been happier about this. It became a bonding moment for them both, and Lydia loved it.

Lydia did not believe in what the priest was telling people at mass. She believed what her heart told her during the hours spent in that sacred space, she believed in the power of connection to life and this supported Lydia in her journey through her dark times. This connection turned out to be her life saver in many ways, for many years.

Christmas 1979 was gloomy and passed quickly. Lydia and her family and grandparents visited Uncle Marvin and his family for the holidays, but Lydia was told that her uncle and aunt were getting a divorce. This was terrible news. Lydia was witnessing life happen around her but had started to feel as though she could not care less.

Her father did not like her grandparents and it seemed that the feeling was mutual. Sergiu claimed that Granddad George was an alcoholic, but this was untrue. Her dear grandfather only drank wine or, at parties, *tuica*, a special brew made from fermented prunes. It is true that when he did drink he quickly became tipsy, but he knew when to stop. Sergiu also voiced his opinion on Valery, telling Lydia that her grandma was too nosy. Maybe she was, but Lydia liked going to see them. Her father didn't want Lydia to continue these visits and he made sure his wishes were understood and obeyed. Lydia remembered what happened when she did not do as she was told, and had no desire to repeat the experience, therefore she stopped visiting her grandparents after school.

Lydia understood full well that her father didn't want her to talk about her life at home. It was best to obey without questioning, and she did.

Her mother worked day shifts at the museum and sometimes, Lydia went to see her. Surprisingly enough, especially considering that she didn't particularly enjoy history at school, being at the museum turned out to be fascinating. It was big and it had many rooms with interesting pieces on display, and Lydia soon became familiar with the place. But this too had to stop.

Lydia became frustrated that everything she enjoyed doing was taken away from her. She shut down even more and decided not show anybody her true feelings.

One day, during PE, there was a man standing next to the track noting the students with the best scores in sprinting, jumping, long-distance running and so on. At the end he took Lydia and several of her classmates aside and asked them if they would like to train with his athletics team. He told the children to speak to their parents about it and have them contact him through the school's PE department.

Beginnings

Lydia went home that day full of enthusiasm. She enjoyed jumping and she liked the idea that she could be good at sports, but she downplayed the situation to her parents, trying to hide her feelings in the hope that she would therefore get her wish.

Unfortunately, it was not to be. Her father and mother decided that she would be better off without it and declined the offer.

'Well,' said Sergiu, 'since you don't seem to be enthusiastic about it, it's probably best to not consider it.'

Instead, he offered to teach her how to play chess.

'Exercising the mind is what you need, Lydia,' he said, from his place at the dinner table where Lydia had brought up the conversation. And the decision was final.

So her strategy of not showing off her true feelings seemed to have backfired. Instead of running and jumping and exercising outdoors, Lydia would get to play chess. Yippee she thought to herself – the gift that keeps on giving.

Sergiu started teaching Lydia that very night. And Lydia hated it. At first. They played with pawns, endless games of pawns, chasing after one another with the same limited moves. They played every afternoon once Lydia had finished her homework. Then it dawned on Lydia: if she asked to play chess the time would then fly by until her mother came back home. This was a bit of a victory, Lydia told herself. Of course, it didn't last long because if one wants to find time one does. And Sergiu most definitely did.

So on top of everything else, Lydia had to put up with chess from that day on.

Lydia's Journey

Throughout her teenage years Lydia's journey fell into a routine once again. She learned how to underplay, how to pretend, how to live a double life. She taught herself to show the world what the world wanted to see, and kept who she truly was to herself. She started to create an outer layer of considerable thickness which prevented her from expressing her true self in public. She was cheerful and she was known and celebrated for her academic performance, yet she did not allow herself to show any feelings about the circumstances at home. She created a protective shield around herself which, in time, became her own, private cage. Many years later and through hours of therapy, she finally understood her double confinement. Yet in those early days, it was the best way Lydia found to deal with her experiences.

After months of being at home and suffering with depression, Sergiu finally appeared to have recovered and went back to play as a first cellist player in Ploiesti's philharmonic orchestra.

Every Tuesday night Harriet, Lydia and Liviu attended the concerts in the big theatre in town. Lydia didn't enjoy this much. Her brother was not keen either, he became impatient easily. Some nights the music was entertaining but mostly uninteresting.

Winter 1980 was particularly hard. Endless snow falls and heavy winds and the cold was bone-shattering. They had to stay indoors for most of the day. After months of knee-deep snow and thick layers of ice everywhere, the first buds of snowdrops finally started to show, the ice began to melt, and the sun rays were getting warmer.

How amazing to witness nature springing to life again!

The scent of freesias and hyacinths in the air, bluebells

Beginnings

in the churchyard where Lydia attended mass with her grandma, the birds coming back to their old nests – everything was signalling to Lydia that life goes on no matter what.

Easter came with the painting of eggs, the baking of buns, the school break, the midnight rituals in church – all was there again, for Lydia to bask in and look forward to.

The blooming trees, the blades of grass, the birdsong and especially the blue skies cheered Lydia up and supported her in her journey. And after the Easter break was over Lydia went back to school and routine took over her days once more.

Step by step and day by day, this would be Lydia's biggest secret in life.

That summer her grandparents took a trip to George's hometown and Lydia was promised a visit to the Black Sea, her favourite summer holiday, on their return.

The first night her grandparents were away, Lydia's mother received a phone call from Valery. Lydia sensed something was wrong from the way her mother had to sit down after the first seconds, how her shoulders began to sag, her demeanour was screaming to Lydia that something terribly bad had happened. Once the conversation was over, Harriet hung up and started crying. She had to catch her breath before she was able to gather her thoughts and let the family know that Granddad George, had just passed away. Harriet had to go and pick up her mother and make arrangements for the remains of her father to be brought back home and buried in the family plot in the cemetery. Lydia stood there next to her mother and

Lydia's Journey

could not contain her tears. They trickled silently down her cheeks, and she felt a void in her heart.

Harriet left that night. She drove four hours through the dark roads and returned the next day with Valery and the body of George.

Lydia spent the next few days in a daze, sadness and helplessness were her main companions. She hugged her grandma tightly, and sat in silence next to her. Orthodox rituals meant they had a wake which allowed the family to spend a few days saying goodbye to their departed loved one in the comfort of their home. Granddad George lay in an open coffin on the table in the living room and family members and friends took turns to sit in the room, remembering fragments of their life together.

George had a weak heart; Lydia already knew this. She had seen him struggle to climb up the few stairs to the apartment, she had witnessed how, little by little, he did less outdoors and spent more time at home or on the bench in front of the main door of the building, playing draughts with friends and neighbours. But Lydia never realised how serious it was until the day she saw him lying in that coffin, lifeless and looking peaceful as though he was asleep. In that moment Lydia understood that Granddad was gone, that he would not be able to listen to her or talk to her ever again. A deep sense of finality took over Lydia with such a power that she felt her shoulders drop under the burden of the imminent change in her reality. Granddad had departed the body lying in that coffin.

Many people loved George. Old colleagues, friends from the neighbourhood, there was a continual stream of people who came to his coffin to say their goodbyes.

The funeral was emotional. Lydia stood in the cemetery's

Beginnings

chapel, dressed in white, not comprehending how life could go on without her granddad. People looked disapprovingly at her and her white clothing rather than the traditional mourning colour of black. Lydia did not like being the centre of attention, especially not in a circumstance such this, and she started to regret her colour choice that day. She remembered that it was her father's recommendation – then his demand – that she wore this outfit. Harriet didn't say anything about Sergiu's decision on Lydia's clothes; she just shook her head and walked away.

After the ceremony people gathered at Valery's home for refreshments, as was customary. At first it did not seem right to Lydia to sit and eat and drink when a beloved family member had just left this world, but when she entered the apartment and found all the people there, she felt grateful she was not alone in those moments. Uncle Marvin was there, Maribel and John too. And to Lydia's surprise, her Uncle Kosta had been allowed to return to the country – he was a fugitive after all – to attend his father's funeral.

A couple of days later, Kosta had to return to Germany. Grandma Val was sad all the time and Lydia couldn't bear seeing her so forlorn. She spoke to Harriet who agreed that Lydia could stay with her grandmother for a few nights. Lydia wanted to live with her grandma permanently, but she knew this was not to be. Nevertheless, Lydia was happy to be back for a short while and to be given a break from her own personal nightmare. Sergiu was not happy but this time Harriet had insisted and got her way.

That summer Lydia had a break from Ploiesti and her everyday life. Grandma decided to spend some weeks

Lydia's Journey

with one of George's relatives who owned a B&B in a town built around a lake known for its therapeutic muds. She took Lydia, Maribel and Liviu along. Harriet came too but Sergiu only stayed for a couple of days before he left. Oh, happy days!

Lydia was covered head to toe in the therapeutic mud that Valery would apply to her skin. It was so cold at first but then it dried and got very hot, until it cracked open like an egg. It stank so terribly that Lydia wanted to vomit. The best part was washing it off in the lake.

A couple of days after Sergiu had gone home, Lydia and Maribel came back from the lake to be introduced to some new arrivals at their host's B&B: a family with three sons, two around Lydia and Maribel's age and a younger brother Liviu's age. That night, under their covers, the girls giggled about the two boys next door, it felt thrilling to Lydia. Maribel liked the brunette and Lydia the blond. So, there was no arguing about that. They fell asleep happy and excited about the next day.

Morning arrived with the sun shining through the open windows and the birds chirping.

Lydia and Maribel were awake early which surprised Valery. They walked out of their room and went to help their host in the outdoor kitchen. She had baked homemade bread which smelled delicious.

Lydia and Maribel helped set the table under the newly-erected awning by the climbing vineyard and they gladly got their hands busy. The boys and their family showed up shortly after and Lydia felt butterflies in her stomach.

The boy with brown hair was called Adrian and the blond Cristian. Maribel seemed nervous too, but they had made

BEGINNINGS

a pact the night before: not to let their family know about their intention to befriend the boys.

It was a relaxed atmosphere, everyone sat at the table and chatted. The families got to know each other, and it turned out that they were distant relatives of Granddad George on his mother's side.

After breakfast they decided to spend the day together at the beach – Lydia and Maribel were delighted. Everyone packed their bags and headed off. The lake was a twenty-minute walk from their residence, and they all made the journey together.

Needless to say, all four had a wonderful time together that summer.

Cristian impressed Lydia with his gentle soul and his willingness to help her with the small chores around their B&B. The policy of the place was that everyone who stayed there would help to keep the place clean and looked after, and help the owner, a short, stocky and cheerful woman called Dorena, to harvest vegetables from her garden or to bring water from the well to the table.

Both girls enjoyed that summer like never before and the company had a lot to do with it. Lydia kept the memory of her first crush on a boy buried deep in her heart. Puppy love, as it is called, is one that is treasured for its purity of emotions.

The summer ended and they said their goodbyes.

Whatever became of Adrian and Cristian, Lydia never knew. But what she was aware of was her father's opinion on how young girls such as herself ought to stay away from boys their age or older.

'Because trouble will happen if you don't,' warned Sergiu with a stern look.

Although Lydia understood by now how joyful moments in her life would be muddied and taken away by her father, she had not expected her mother to inform him of her crush on Cristian, and she began to realise that Harriet might be more than just a secondary actor in this big, messy situation. Unexpected feelings of resentment towards her started digging their roots into Lydia's heart.

Lydia decided to no longer obey her mother. And so began her disdainful behaviour towards her. If Harriet asked her to go to the shop, Lydia would say no. When Harriet asked her daughter to wash the dishes, Lydia would offer the same answer.

Surprisingly, Sergiu did not punish Lydia for this behaviour towards her mother. This taught Lydia another lesson: she could become her father's ally and punish her mother for the role she chose to play – in Germany, on the journey to the river when she disregarded Lydia's plea for help. From that moment she saw a new way of relating to the members of her family and Lydia made it her mission to understand her father and his depression, to try and help him which in turn would obviously please him and hopefully make things easier on her.

Her father was certainly pleased, but he did not stop his visits as Lydia had hoped. She had to continue to play the game of chess, and of life.

That year, her mathematics teacher, Miss Oana Munteanu set up a chess competition for the pupils. She often said that maths and chess were related and if one is good at maths, then one ought to be good at playing chess too.

Beginnings

Lydia met her adversaries and one by one, she defeated them. Quite a buzz generated around her. The teacher's favourite student, a boy called Alexander, was also good and Lydia began to understand that Miss Oana was biased towards him. Being so competitive, Lydia could not help herself from wanting to win the chess competition.

Sergiu was surprised when one day Lydia came to him to ask for more insights into the game and how to defeat Alexander. Her father helped her.

The finals came and the whole class crowded round Lydia and Alexander who were sitting opposite each other at a desk. Like true competitors they shook hands before the game and full of assertiveness and confidence, Alexander said:

'And may the best chess player win,' with an undertone that suggested that everyone in the room knew who that would be.

As they started the game and made their moves. Lydia felt inspired, as though she had played this very game before. She discovered that she could anticipate Alexander's moves, and she won. No big deal. But it was a big deal!

'Well, Lydia,' said the teacher, 'if you are so skilled at chess, I wonder why that doesn't translate into being just as good at maths.' What a cruel thing to say to someone who just won a competition!

'I guess I don't like maths as much as I like chess,' answered Lydia, and it felt good to finally get that off her chest.

Miss Oana stood there speechless looking at her pupil.

Lydia's Journey

Lydia went home that day with a huge smile on her face and gave her father the good news.

And her father felt generous enough to give her his reward.

Days turned into weeks, months and years. Every day was the same.

Lydia found joy in the little things: the sunrises and sunsets, the short chats she had with her classmate Octavian on their bus ride home. The Sundays in church with Grandma Val and the family dinners at Christmas and Easter.

Summers were no longer joyful because Sergiu decided the family should take trips to the countryside. He justified this by saying that it was good for his nerves. They drove out of the city, pitched a tent by the river and then Sergiu did what he did best: bark orders at everybody.

'Gather fire for night time!'

'Peel the scales from the fish and cook them over the fire!"

'Clean the bowls and the plates by the river!'

Lydia enjoyed nature greatly but hated these holidays. She couldn't help but remember her grandmother Maria, Sergiu's mother, propped up in the bed against her cushions. She also suffered with a delicate nervous constitution. But she didn't go out in nature nor sleep in a tent. There were no comforts during these trips. At night they had to take turns to sit by the fire and make sure no wild animal intruded. *Not fun, not necessary*, Lydia thought.

However, one of those trips turned out to be completely and wonderfully different. It was summer 1981 and

Beginnings

instead of driving down south to the river Danube, Sergiu announced that they would take a trip through the Carpathian mountains, visiting monasteries, castles and museums.

They set off in the morning and slept the first night in the minivan, after a long sixteen-hour drive from Ploiesti, heading north-west towards the region of Ramnicu Valcea. They parked by the gates of the first monastery on their route: Curtea de Arges. Built between 1515 and 1517 in a Byzantine style, the centrepiece of this monastery, the Cathedral Curtea de Arges, showed itself the following morning, its splendour bathed in the sunlight. It was stunning to watch the light reflecting from its tall roofs above the white stone walls.

They were only allowed to admire this man-made beauty from the grounds because Sergiu, who did not believe in God, also turned out to not believe in human creation and he refused to pay for tickets to visit the interior. It was beautiful and Lydia loved being on sacred grounds. She could feel the difference in vibrations, the energy of the place and she opened her heart to welcome it.

They wandered around inside the precinct, watched the monks going about their day and wondered at some of the ancient building preserved inside the walls, then had a frugal meal back at the minivan before they continued their journey.

This monastery was situated at the feet of the impressive Carpathian mountains. They started the journey on the road up that beautiful expression of natural creation, on a dual carriageway flanked on the right-hand side by tall trees and small rivulets rolling their crystalline waters into the valley, and by the drop of the growing mountain side on the left.

Lydia's Journey

They stopped several times and finally, as the day moved into the evening and the light began to fade quickly, Sergiu decided to find a place to camp. They took one of the mountain dirt roads to get away from the traffic and found a spot, near a small river, wide and flat enough to park and set a campfire on. The night came and went, and despite some nocturnal noises and Sergiu's suspicions that something or someone was watching them, nothing happened and they packed the car in the morning and resumed their journey.

They reached the top of the mountain around midday and stopped at the edge of a deep glacier lake – Balea. It looked majestic: green waters against the dark blue sky and rocky mountain tips in the distance. Taking in that rich, cold, mountain air made Lydia slightly dizzy, but she was so humbled standing there, the lake waters at her feet, the sky above her, admiring the magnificence of nature. It was a lesson of resilience that life had presented to her, and Lydia took it to her heart. She came down the other side of the mountain a different person. A resilient young girl who would carry on until she found a way out.

The trip was inspiring. The villages along the road, the water wells where women spun the wheel to pull up the bucket full of cold, clean water, the bakeries which prepared delicious buns for the road, the museums, the historical sites and the castles they visited, all packed in a very busy schedule which they managed to complete in a little over three weeks.

They arrived back home, and the magic faded as soon as Lydia stepped into the apartment.

The upcoming school year was the one which would decide Lydia's future – or at least is what her mother told her. At the end of the year Lydia would have to choose

Beginnings

which high school curriculum she wanted to pursue in preparation for her future career.

The schooling system in Romania, back then, was structured into primary then secondary school for every child up to the age of fourteen. At the end of secondary school students had to choose a college based upon the career path they had decided to take. There were examinations at the end of secondary school and the more demanding the curriculum of the chosen high school, the more challenging the admission criteria was.

Most of Lydia's classmates prepared for the exams under the supervision of private tutors. The subjects were mathematics, including algebra and geometry, and Romanian language and literature.

Uncle Marvin was charged with preparing Lydia for the mathematics. For Romanian language and literature, her grandma had the perfect person: a retired teacher, sought after by many parents given her high rates of success in tuition. She was called Miss Draganescu and Lydia came to love her because of her sharp mind and pre-prepared essays.

September came and Lydia's last year at secondary school commenced. Uncle Marvin met Lydia at her grandma's apartment twice a week, and they sat at the dining table, books open, pencils sharp and ready to go. Uncle Marvin loved mathematics, and he wanted to inspire the same passion in Lydia. He was a quick thinker, fast in finding solutions to problems – Lydia would witness some heavy defeats of her father when he played chess with Uncle Marvin. But Lydia didn't like this pressure during his tutoring. They were different characters and they clashed. Lydia grew to hate Uncle Marvin's style of teaching and she refused to continue. Her parents allowed her to stop

Lydia's Journey

on the condition that she would learn on her own because they could not afford a second private tutor. But the decision raised serious concern about Lydia's potential success in the end-of -year exams.

Lydia herself did not seem worried. She was determined to succeed and she focused on the task. Before the Christmas break, Lydia and her closest friend challenged each other to solve 400 maths problems by the end of the holiday and bring the completed exercises to school on the first day of term in January.

Christmas came. The tree was back in the living room, shining and glittering, but the house was extremely cold because of a shortage of electricity and gas imposed by the government. Lydia was not interested in politics and only observed the commentaries exchanged by her family around the dining table. It seemed that the government was struggling with external debts, so had reduced energy supply for the entire country. Which meant that all households in Romania from 1982 onwards had only two hours of heating and two hours of television a day. Lydia started to wear her winter jacket, woollen scarf and gloves inside the apartment, while doing her homework. That year candlelight was back in fashion, but that didn't put Lydia off loving candles.

She was very proud of herself in January, when she went back to school carrying her maths notebook with 400 solved problems and exercises. And so did her friend. Lydia considered the challenge to be a success because it served both girls well in preparation for their exams in June.

Beginnings

Lydia started with Miss Draganescu in January and every week after her hour of tuition, she would walk back home with a new essay which she had to learn by heart for her next class.

Essays started to pile up in her brain, math equations and geometrical shapes haunted her dreams. Finally, her father gave her a break from his visits and allowed her to start doing her homework in her own bedroom, moving Liviu to do his in his parent's room.

This certainly helped Lydia. She locked herself in her bedroom for as long as there was enough daylight, then she moved into the living room with the rest of her family to continue by candlelight. She became so focused and close to obsessed with her studies that she had no thoughts other than succeeding in the upcoming exams.

The weeks seemed to fly by, and her progress was noticeable both in school and in her private lessons.

Around May 1983, Lydia's father started to exhibit symptoms of depression once again. Harriet seemed to have less and less patience, even in her interactions with Liviu, which started to concern Lydia.

One Saturday afternoon, Lydia's father informed her that they were to spend the next day together, on a bike ride in the countryside. On Sunday, at 4 a.m., they left on their bikes. Sergiu had a regular bicycle while Lydia's was a racing model with three different speeds.

It was still dark outside and the streets were empty and quiet. They took the road leading east out of Ploiesti and soon left the city's streetlights behind, heading into the traffic that had started to gather. They rode through villages and small towns, putting more and more distance between themselves and home.

Lydia had no idea where her father was taking her, nor of his plans for the day. The only thing to do was to keep pedalling until eventually they would be pedalling their way back home.

Around midday, they finally reached what Lydia assumed to be their destination. A river, not very impressive, outside Buzau. They sat down on the riverbank. There were no trees to give shelter from the midday sun, nor any type of vegetation as Lydia had seen alongside other water sources. This river seemed barren. Sergiu was particularly quiet and Lydia didn't like it. She preferred it when he talked to her, his silence reminded her of him sitting and staring at the wall, and she feared her father when he was like that. They began to pull out sandwiches and water bottles from their backpacks, and in the quiet air, thick with dust from the field behind them and the smell of rubber from a factory nearby, they began to eat. It was a desolate landscape and Lydia wondered why her father had chosen this river, when there were so many other beautiful sites surrounding Ploiesti. After they ate and drank and rested for a couple of hours, they started to prepare for the bike ride back. And that is when it started. It was the first time Lydia witnessed an anxiety attack. Sergiu became agitated and started mumbling to himself. He began to breathe quickly and when Lydia looked into his eyes, she saw fear in them. His breath became shallower by the minute, and he could not calm down. He became increasingly disturbed. Lydia was at a loss.

'You have to go now, Lydia, I need you to get me help,' he said.

Beginnings

Lydia looked at him puzzled, she had no idea what to do.

'Where do I go?' she asked.

'You'll have to figure that out on your own, use your brain, I need you to get me help.'

Lydia looked at Sergiu and hoped that he was joking, but he wasn't. His face was stern, and Lydia thought that he had lost his marbles.

In hindsight, Sergiu's mental health condition meant he was losing his grip on reality.

Lydia picked up her bike and walked up to the dirt road leading to the dual carriageway they had come from. She mounted the bike and looked behind at her father, but he was pacing up and down the river not paying attention to her.

Lydia started pedalling, she would ride back to Ploiesti – about ninety kilometres away – and ask her mother to go and collect her father.

At least she had a plan. She started her journey back. But the further she cycled away from her father, the more alone and scared she started to become. She felt thirsty, so she had to stop. After taking a short sip from her water bottle she got back on the road. Then she felt hungry. So she stopped again, this time getting off her bike and sitting down on the grass alongside the road to eat a sandwich. From the corner of her eye, she made out a tiny figure who reminded her of her father. When she looked closer, it was her father. He pedalled fast, approached her, and passed her without even a hint of recognition in his face. She packed her bag quickly and jumped on her bike to try to catch up with him. Which eventually, she did. When she fell in line behind him, Sergiu started to slow down a bit, motioning to her with his left hand, asking her to come alongside him. Checking to make sure no cars were coming, Lydia did so.

'I can't afford to stop. We have to keep going until we are back home. So, keep moving and don't delay me.'

Roger that, she answered in her head.

They kept going. It was early afternoon, and Lydia knew that it was going to be a very long ride back home.

She had started slowing down when her father prompted her from the front.

'Find a song to match your pace and keep singing it in your head,' he said loudly.

So she did. And it worked quite well, until she started to feel her muscles giving up under the amount of lactic acid produced by all her effort. But she had to keep going.

The sun was setting behind the treetops. The air was beginning to feel chilly, and Lydia wanted to throw the bike in the bin and lay down on the grass. She suggested sleeping on the side of the road for a couple of hours, but her father made it clear that this was not an option. The chill of the night, the moisture of the grass and them not having sleeping bags would result in pneumonia and death. For a moment, to Lydia, death seemed less cruel than her father.

The night closed in on them and the car lights were blinding an exhausted Lydia who just wished this ride through hell would end. She could no longer make out her father's silhouette in front of her. They were pedalling through the last thirty kilometres of hills before reaching Ploiesti, a vineyard spread for as far as the eye could see. But Lydia was drained and could not, mentally, emotionally or physically, push another foot on those pedals. She decided to stop and take a break. She got off and started walking uphill, dragging the bike on her left side, on the road. Her father came back after her but not even him and his threats of punishment could motivate Lydia to climb back on her bike.

'I would rather walk my way back, than put a foot on these pedals once more, no matter how long it takes,' she said, stubborn and defiant.

Her father looked at her and finally found a way to arouse her competitive spirit, her need to prove herself.

'If you stop now your muscles will cramp up and you will not be able to continue and get back home on your own. You will have failed to achieve your goal. You will not reach home on your own,' and he turned around and rode away, leaving Lydia behind.

Through the fogginess of her pain and exertion, she could envision the defeat her father predicted, and she awoke for the last sprint. She climbed back on her bicycle and started pedalling until she noticed her father waiting further down the road for her to catch up. They arrived back home around 2 a.m. on Monday. Harriet and Valery were waiting for them. Valery openly questioned Sergiu's responsibilities towards his daughter during such an important year for her and Lydia had to admire her grandma's fiesty spirit. Nobody dared talk to her father like that and Sergiu was caught by surprise. He looked at Valery, standing there in front of him with a stern look in her eyes and not an inch intimidated by his tall figure. Sergiu was speechless and he turned on his heels and went to the bedroom. Grandma Val left shortly after and four hours later, when Lydia woke up to go to school, she realised that she could not move. Her muscles were too tight and sore to obey her brain's command and she had to spend the entire day in bed.

But she had to concede that her father had been right about her: she could not contemplate defeat brought about by her own actions. And she felt very proud of her achievement, of her ability to overcome physical exertion that night.

It took Lydia over a week to finally recover from the effort and release the pain in her muscles.

She went back to school two days after that infamous Sunday and Grandma never came back to their house again until years later after Sergiu had left for Spain.

The exams were approaching and Lydia felt the pressure of the expectations placed upon her increase.

Miss Draganescu was pleased with her progress and Lydia felt confident that she would do well in maths too. Uncle Marvin gave her a mock test, about two months before the exam and he declared, to his surprise, that Lydia was indeed ready. That encouraged Lydia to continue with her programme, she was reassured by her uncle's assessment.

Lydia had to choose the subject she wanted to pursue next year, and her mother suggested she follow a path which would bring her satisfaction and financial stability. Harriet argued for Lydia to apply to the only high school in town which offered a nursing degree. Lydia would thus achieve both: her high school diploma and the degree which would qualify her for a nursing job anywhere in the field.

Beginnings

'Besides,' continued Harriet, 'it will give you the opportunity to find out if you want to follow the path of a medical university degree and you will have more inside knowledge of the human body if you do decide to go to medical school afterwards.'

It all seemed to make sense and Lydia was one to follow logic. So she decided to apply to the Ploiesti Health High School, also known as Ploiesti Nursing College.

It had one of the most challenging admission criteria in the city. The year Lydia signed up, there were four hundred and thirty-two applications for just seventy-two places. Lydia would have to be the best out of a total of six students per seat, she had to outrun five of those who would compete for her place. It was tough competition.

Lydia increased the fire in her burners and gave her all.

The week before the exam, she had memorised seventy-five different essays, each between three and six A4 pages long. She was able to recite them in her dreams, which at times did happen. She ate essays, breathed essays, regurgitated them at will while on the bus ride home from school.

In maths she kept solving problems and exercises and finally, when she began to feel fed up with it all, the day of the first of the two exams arrived.

First was mathematics. It was four hours long, in a big classroom full of students just like her.

She didn't look around, didn't make eye contact. She had her own butterflies to contend with and she did her best.

When she got out that day, her mother, and grandmother were waiting for her by the gates of the big building. She went home with them in silence. She was in the zone and wanted to keep her concentration levels up for the next day.

The following day came and went and now, on her way back home with Grandma Val and her mother, Lydia felt empty, depleted, flat.

The waiting period had begun, and Lydia knew that her results would be released in the next couple of weeks.

Funny how the same number of seconds do seem to pass with different speed, depending on the expectation attached to them.

At last Lydia's wait was over and one sunny day in July, she woke up and remembered that today was the day she would find out her results.

She got up and dressed and joined her mother in the kitchen for breakfast. She sat in silence. Filled with anticipation, she couldn't utter a word. Terrified that she might fail because she had no back up. A place at that school was all she wanted. There was no plan B, no safety net. It was all or nothing.

Harriet stood up and they both got ready to leave the house to collect Grandma.

They took the bus to the town centre and approached the school. There was already a large number of parents and students, crowded by the windows which exhibited the results on four pieces of A4 paper.

All three approached the building and started to look at the list.

The names were numbered, according to their results, and

Beginnings

Harriet started looking for Lydia's name from number seventy-two upwards.

Valery went straight to the top of the list.

'You're in! My darling, you are in!' she shrilled and she turned around to Lydia, to make room for her to get close to the window and take a look.

'Where am I?' asked Lydia. She could barely make out the names, the writing was small, and Lydia was not very tall.

'You are number six, my dear, number six from the top, my sweetheart,' said her grandma with love and pride, in a loud voice so everybody around them could hear. Heads turned to look at them, curious to see who got so high up in the list.

Lydia overflowed with joy. A massive sigh of relief left her chest and her mother hugged her after Valery finally released Lydia from her own embrace.

She had made it! She had proven to herself and those who knew her that she could achieve her goals, in spite of competition and pressure.

Uncle Marvin joined in to give Lydia the family acknowledgement she deserved. Since Maribel had also been admitted into a high-achieving high school, both girls were celebrated, and Sergiu could find no reason to prevent Lydia from attending the party. He did, however, refuse to go to the restaurant himself. Lydia remembered her mother saying that he did not feel very well and preferred to stay home, his nervous disposition being so … delicate.

The pat on the back from her father accompanied by a

'well done' contrasted with the more effusive expression of joy from her mother; Liviu was considered to be too young to understand therefore he was not expected to congratulate his sister.

Lydia felt very proud of her results. Exhausted, depleted, but enormously proud. A deep sense of accomplishment washed over her and she understood that she could transform any of her dreams into reality with the right leverage and preparation.

She was fourteen years old, and she felt the fire of her desires burning inside her. She wanted to be heard. She wanted the world to see her, to listen to her. She wanted to be accepted and loved for who she was.

But who she was terrified Lydia.

In that moment of intense happiness, Lydia was struck by the fact that the world did not know what she knew: she was a deceitful teenager who led a double life. There was the life that everyone knew and the one which had to be kept hidden. In that moment of triumph and glory, Lydia dragged herself down, blamed herself for the reality of her life experiences and turned the sweet flavour of success into a thorn of guilt and a bitter reminder that she had to lay low and see where the path would take her.

Chapter 4

'In life, there is no right or wrong decision, only that which aligns you with the purpose of your existence, or not.'

Lydia, 2021

High school finally started, and Lydia couldn't believe she was about to take her first steps towards a career in medicine.

The school uniform was different and the new school community was much smaller. It felt like she had moved into a select group of students, a sort of VIP club.

The classroom was in a Victorian-style building with high ceilings and tall windows. It was cold during the winter and hot in the summer. She entered the room and she found that all but one of her classmates were girls.

The school had only twelve male students in total, something Lydia was not used to at all.

Her parents, on the other hand, found this acceptable

Lydia's Journey

and even considered it to be reassuring, as her mother suggested that first night at dinner.

'It reduces distractions, my dear.'

Lydia looked into her bowl, concentrating on the delicious noodles in her soup.

New school, new teachers, new routine. Lydia was excited. She was looking forward to starting her training to become a nurse.

The introductions were made, and the school year began.

It was a step up from what Lydia had been used to at school. She was introduced to medical instruments, to the many components of a metal-glass syringe and how to use it, on an orange at first. She learned about diseases and how to recognise them. She was taught about the basics of a hospital and the many departments it could house. The first semester of Nursing College was about the theory of nursing. But after that, it became a mixture of theory and practice – the first three weeks of each month was academic study, the same as every other high school in the country, while the fourth week was spent in the hospital wards. The real contact with the hospital environment began.

Lydia remembered her first day as a trainee nurse. They gathered in the basement of one of the town's major hospitals at 6.30 a.m. and changed into their uniforms – a white, three-quarter-length medical coat with their name embroidered on the left upper pocket. At 7 a.m. the instructor took the group of fifteen people upstairs onto the main floor and scattered them throughout the wards.

Their first day was about record keeping – being there

Beginnings

during the consultants' visits and listening carefully, taking notes of all that was going on. Lydia loved this part of the training. Yet she found the medical side and the regular high school learning overwhelming, until she got used to the new system.

Her new colleagues were of a different breed. The fact that they had all been admitted into this select group fed their egos and Lydia found it difficult to relate to them, given her own circumstances at home. Yet she remained hopeful that she could find somebody on her wavelength who she could befriend.

Mathematics was impossible and not even Uncle Marvin could help. She enjoyed physics but the teacher was extremely strict and old school. Lydia regarded her as a challenge, and she started to pay special attention to the subject. No student had ever got a mark higher than seven out of ten and Lydia's grades began to approach this benchmark until one day, towards the end of the first term, she received a nine. Her classmates were ecstatic, if a little jealous, and Lydia had proven to herself once again that she could achieve whatever she set out to do.

Before the end of the term, she would even score a ten and her teacher became very interested in Lydia's potential.

But Lydia's motive had been to prove a point, to show that she could achieve a high mark if she wanted to, not because she was interested in learning physics in depth. After she had achieved these high grades, her interest diminished, and she went back to the same scores as most of her classmates. Her teacher was most disappointed in Lydia. Yet Lydia did not seem to care.

Lydia's Journey

She began to change. Her teenage years were rough waters to navigate, and Lydia was faced with many challenges. Some she had to adjust course to overcome, some proved to be very difficult while others, plain impossible.

In early 1984 Uncle Kosta, who still lived in Germany, died at the age of forty-four. The entire family was devastated. He had a beautiful daughter named Hannah, who was just three years old when her father died.

Grandma Val was allowed to travel to West Germany for her son's funeral. Kosta had died of a heart attack, apparently the same kind that had killed his father, four short years earlier.

Valery came back to Romania a different person. She would wear the black of mourning for many years to come and Lydia did not know what to do to help her. It broke her heart to see her grandma in so much pain. Not that Lydia had an easy life either.

Sergiu had become more present and more persistent, and Lydia resigned herself to ignorance because she did not know what else to do.

Valery asked Harriet once again to allow Lydia to sleep at her apartment and Lydia went there for a few nights, but it became more difficult for her to keep her thoughts to herself. In the end, Lydia didn't want to stay there any longer because she feared that she could not keep quiet about her shameful hidden life experiences for long.

How could Lydia keep going, keep pretending, keep smiling when everything around her was falling apart? She had an acute sense of a terrible loss; she could not shake the inevitability of her circumstances and she did not know how to escape.

Beginnings

She rebelled against her mother by neglecting her household chores and by declining any assistance when asked and yet all was forgiven, which infuriated Lydia even more. She sank into her own depression, unseen and unheard. She stopped taking showers every day and would only grudgingly bathe when strongly requested and loudly admonished for the strong scent which trailed her. She stopped grooming herself and outside school she wore boys' clothing – large trousers and baggy shirts. She did her best to look repulsive and scruffy.

She could barely look at her body. She hated it. They did not have large mirrors in the house, but even when brushing her teeth she could hardly stand to see her reflection in the bathroom mirror. Nobody stopped to question what was going on with her. Everyone was looking elsewhere.

When Lydia remembers those days, she often asks herself if all adults are the same, if all parents would choose to see what they wanted, or what was convenient for them in their children. As an adult, and especially as a mother, Lydia could not understand how Harriet did not notice the signs. They were there, in plain sight. And yet unexplained.

By the age of fifteen, Lydia was so concerned about how to spend a night safely in her bed that her grades started to suffer. She became a mediocre student, who would score highly once in a while. Her mother wasn't like Grandma Val. She seemed to accept Lydia's grades without concern. Liviu was an average student and he was not to be sanctioned for it either. Because 'boys develop later in life,' her mother kept telling Lydia.

Lydia's Journey

Lydia spent her studies at home trying to catch up, rather than excel. She convinced herself during her first years of school that knowledge mattered more than grades but that was an idea in which she no longer believed. She embraced the white coat training as if it were her salvation raft and she did her best in the rest of her assignments.

She knew that at the end of her second high school year there was another exam, based on specific subjects, more difficult than the admission exam, and she began to worry. Lydia could not afford to photocopy an entire textbook so she resorted to her own artistic skills to reproduce it.

She asked for permission from the librarian to borrow the school's anatomy book for the summer and she started to copy it, word by word, page by page and picture by picture. It turned into a beautifully handwritten book, with black and white pen drawings of cells, bones, the human skeleton, muscles. Lydia would treasure that book for what it meant more than for its content.

Other than this project, summer that year also brought a trip to the mountains with Sergiu towards the end of August. Harriet and Liviu had been invited but both politely declined.

This time, thank goodness, Lydia would not have to ride her bike. Instead, they travelled by car to the foot of the mountain where they camped – in a proper tent, this time – before the climbing began the next day.

The following morning, before dawn, Lydia and Sergiu packed the tent into the car then prepared their backpacks with their sleeping bags and some pots for cooking and tools for gathering firewood. Then they started their ascent along the footpath. It was a beautiful day, it had an

Beginnings

autumnal feel, although it was still August. The trees had started to change colour slightly and the air was fresh and full of the fragrance of earth and moss.

The footpath seemed quite worn at first but the higher they climbed, the narrower it became. Lydia found the forest invigorating. She focused her attention ahead, on the path, on the sounds of the forest and the sun shining through the high branches of the tall trees. Sometimes she spotted a butterfly, the ones with large wings and dark, rich brown and orange flecks on their wings.

Sergiu talked to her, and she responded, but Lydia was aware of his motives, and she only went along with it to make things easier on herself. Where else would she go? Was there an alternative? Of course there wasn't, and Lydia refused, systematically and stubbornly, to ask herself rhetorical questions. Her experiences tormented her enough, she wasn't going to add even more to her mental, emotional and physical challenges.

The night started to close in, and Sergiu looked for a place to camp. He found a sloped path which led to an elevated platform from where they could look down on the mountain side and the trees growing below. The platform was accessible only from the path. It was a very strategic position – as Sergiu eloquently explained to Lydia – because behind them was the mountain, as if it were cut by a laser, only shy branches of young trees growing horizontally from it. At the edge of the platform and all around it, there was another drop, impossible to climb, so they should be safe to camp there that night. Yet when Sergiu and Lydia looked further up they noticed an opening in the mountain wall which looked like a cave.

'Stay here, Lydia,' ordered Sergiu as he went to investigate the opening.

Lydia's Journey

He returned about five minutes later.

'It seems that we have stumbled upon a bear's cave,' he seemed relaxed and not at all concerned at the prospect of spending the night in front of a bear's house, thought Lydia.

'We should unpack quickly and get as much firewood as we can before nightfall,' he added as he started to take things out of his backpack. Lydia followed his example, even though her mind was screaming at her to leave, to run, to put as much distance as possible between the cave, the bear and the mad man in front of her. Again, she had to force these thoughts to stop and instead she prayed that she would see the coming dawn.

They gathered as much firewood as they could and Sergiu placed as many branches and stones as he could spare along the path to the platform, using the heavier branches to block the access to it. He positioned his sleeping bag against a tall tree flanking the entrance to it. Lydia watched him as she neatly stacked the firewood and when he finished barricading the access to their camp, he sat down and asked Lydia to unpack the canned soup for them to heat up and eat. They started the fire and decided upon a rota to take turns staying awake to listen to the forest and keep the fire going.

Soon night was upon them. The sounds in the forest can be terrifying if one spends it on the ground, with only the flames of a fire for protection.

Sergiu took the first shift and told Lydia to try and sleep. She couldn't. She crawled into her sleeping bag and listened: to the earth, to the air, to the night owls, to the leaves rustling in the wind, high up between the branches.

As she lay there, on her right-hand side and watching the

Beginnings

flames, she felt thumps on the ground with her right ear. She froze. Sergiu moved slightly. The thumping stopped briefly and then started again, sounding and feeling closer.

'Lydia! Get up! NOW!' shouted Sergiu, but Lydia was already up and out of her sleeping bag.

'Grab the saucepans and start making noise!' he demanded. It was what they had planned should this happen.

Lydia grabbed the pans and started crashing them into each other, creating havoc in the forest. Sergiu grabbed his and started too. They yelled their lungs out and smashed those pans until Lydia's hands and ears began to hurt.

Sergiu motioned for Lydia to stop. They listened. The silence was deafening.

Then somewhere down below, there was movement and grunting. Cracking branches and more groans. The thumping started again. The bear was coming back! Lydia stood behind the fire. She fed the flames, and they grew higher. For a second, she thought she saw a silhouette on the path and two glistening sparks in the air, a short distance from the floor and static in their relationship to one another. Like two small, ferocious eyes staring at her. Her heart was beating outside her chest. She started clanging the saucepans with no need for encouragement and her father joined her as he too could make out a shape on the sloped path.

Lydia did not remember how long they stood there making infernal noise. Finally, the bear left. But neither of them could sleep. They spent the rest of the night standing guard and stoking the fire until at last the first rays of daylight started to lighten the treetops. Birds started to

Lydia's Journey

wake up and chirp and Lydia knew that at least in the light, not all cats would look black.

They reached the top of the mountain around noon and decided to climb down via a different path which led them back to their car more quickly. By nightfall, Lydia and Sergiu were well into the outskirts of the village and as the first streetlights started to turn on they had arrived at their car.

It was a short forty-five-minute journey to Ploiesti, and they were relieved to be back in the apartment with Harriet and Liviu that night.

And so the summer ended.

In their second high school year, the college hired the services of Dr Barnescu, a forensic doctor, to take charge of the anatomy curriculum. On his first day he offered the class the opportunity to assist him in performing autopsies at the hospital. His students couldn't believe they had such an awesome opportunity to see inside the human body for themselves. So one Saturday morning the entire class went to witness their first autopsy.

When Lydia arrived the room was rather crowded. She looked around, took in the hospital smells and the clinical look of it all, then rushed to find a good spot to watch the procedure. It had already started, and she managed to make out, over classmates' backs and heads, the open torso and abdomen of a female body. When she looked over to the head, expecting to see the familiar features of a human face, she could barely hide her shock at the sight of a face with the skin rolled back over it. The skull had already been opened.

Beginnings

Her first impression of the autopsy was not what she expected. It made her feel uncomfortable and unsettled but she did not want to admit this to herself or anybody else. It revealed to Lydia the truth of the physical form: it is limited, confined, time bound. The body left behind when the soul takes off, disintegrates. The magic is gone. For a while, Lydia would have nightmares with corpses of the people she loved, envisioning their bodies being open and their entrails inspected.

But for now, she went home that day and told her family the tale of how grateful she was to have a teacher who could introduce them to the mysteries of the human body, which is what she wanted to know as part of her training in her future career.

Her mother was pleased with Lydia's experience. Her father was not fooled.

Lydia continued with her studies, she felt slightly more motivated that year and her grades improved.

In PE, like all her classmates, she struggled. The class was held in a very unorthodox setting: the college did not have a proper gym or modern facilities so they had to rely on the shabby house and grounds of a former student who had passed away years ago and had generously donated their home to the school. The back garden of the small property was the athletics field, while the musty-smelling house was where the pupils did their push ups and similar exercises.

Ploiesti Nursing College was an odd school with odd resources, and Lydia began to question whether she actually liked it or if she would even be able to make it to the end of her course. She had to try, at least, so try she did.

Lydia focused on the benefits for her future career and she found some balance in her daily routine again.

The college was in the town centre – there was a book shop on the way to the bus station and Lydia loved to stop and browse. She had saved some money from her allowance and she began to buy books. She had always loved to read and mostly borrowed from the local or school libraries. But that year, Lydia decided to start building her own book collection and she became a bit of a bookworm. She accumulated more and more books, and she used reading as a means of escaping reality.

Between school, homework, theatre trips on Tuesdays with her parents and Liviu, and sometimes on Sundays with her grandma and Uncle Marvin, Lydia's second year passed uneventfully, and at the end of it she sat her exams. This time Lydia was more interested in simply passing the two four-hour-long sessions, rather than in excelling. And she did pass them, which allowed to her continue, and finish her final years of high school education in the Ploiesti Nursing College.

The last two years had changed Lydia. She had become angry and resentful. Angry at herself and resentful towards her family, the one she grew up with before moving to Germany, the one and only family she would ever consider and who seemed to have vanished into the background a long time ago. Grandma Val seemed to have lost her spark and Uncle Marvin was busy juggling his teaching, private tutoring and coaching his basketball

Beginnings

team, plus seeing his new lady friend who would shortly become his wife. Maribel was busy with her own high school studies and since the divorce of her parents was seen at her father's gatherings or Grandma's Val less and less often.

Lydia's life experiences, especially the secret ones, weighed heavily on her and she began to feel the burden of a lonely journey. She even started to question whether the connection to life she felt through love, was real, as she could no longer feel it. She still went to church, not for solace, but to question. In her mind, while sitting next to her grandmother in church, Lydia would raise her fist to Jesus and ask why he had allowed it to happen. She would question him about what sins she had committed to deserve such a punishment. She finally gave up her rhetorical questions as she received no answer.

Lydia and her family sometimes spent their summer holidays at the Black Sea, and other times they went back to the village where she and Maribel had met Adrian and Cristian. Lydia still found pleasure in the waters and the sand. She still enjoyed the taste of corn on the cob, and she would look at the trinkets and think, *One day, Lydia, one day*.

Lydia's chess playing also improved and although she still did not like the game, she would on occasion win. At first her father let her beat him but then, with patience and perseverance, Lydia began to notice some flaws in his armour and she achieved a small victory. She knew when she won on her own merit, because her father tried to hide his signs of displeasure, just like the ones she recognised from when he lost to Uncle Marvin.

Lydia's Journey

The seasons followed one another and in April 1984, Lydia had to tell her mother that she had been missing her periods. Before she did this, she had told Sergiu. And he gave Lydia permission to discuss it with her mother.

Harriet listened to Lydia in silence and then made an appointment with an obstetrician in town. Her office was in a tall, old-style building and Harriet accompanied Lydia to the examination. After the doctor had carried out her checks she invited Harriet into the examination room and broke the news to both mother and daughter. Lydia was five months pregnant.

Shock and despair hit them. The doctor started to discuss options for the delivery of the baby. She asked Harriet if she wanted the pregnancy to be known in town, to which she received the answer she expected, 'No.' The two women then carried on the conversation as if Lydia was not even there.

Harriet and Lydia left the surgery. Questions filled Lydia's head. But she had been prepared by her father about what to say and she diverted all her mother's questions to Sergiu. He would be the one to tell Harriet about Lydia's 'secret boyfriend' and how he made sure to end their 'relationship' when he found out about Lydia's pregnancy.

Lydia was convinced that the whole secret would blow up in their faces and although she feared the consequences, she relished the potential relief that would come with such a confession.

How mistaken she was!

Lydia's mother stopped quizzing her and instead started sewing a corset for her to wear under her school uniform. She would make sure that Lydia did not show any signs

Beginnings

of pregnancy to the rest of the world for the next four months. Not even to Grandma Val, who started asking questions at family gatherings, but they were quickly shut down by Sergiu. Lydia's father became very protective of her, he stopped Harriet from being sarcastic towards her, and Lydia could not put one foot outside her apartment without his consent and knowledge of her whereabouts. He became like her shadow, and it was obvious to Lydia the reason why: he was afraid that she would find someone to talk to and reveal the truth.

The following four months could not pass quickly enough. As Lydia's pregnancy progressed, so would her difficulty in performing simple tasks such as running for the school bus or doing her abdominal exercises in PE. Her teachers began to question her and as her waistline expanded the headteacher, an elderly and experienced nurse, looked at Lydia with increasingly raised eyebrows, yet she said nothing.

Lydia went to her obstetrician for regular check-ups to assess the progress of her pregnancy and as she lay in her bed at night she wished her life was over. She did not know how much longer she could keep up with her reality: a horrifying nightmare. The pregnancy at least provided some respite from her father's visits, and she grasped at anything that put distance between her and his abuse. By now she was old enough to understand the atrocity of his actions and she was also brave enough to admit that she could have gone to the police and denounced him. But the pregnancy complicated everything, and now she saw herself more as an accomplice rather than a victim. She was made to believe that the pregnancy was her fault and piles of guilt and shame weighed down against her teenage shoulders. It was complicated and Lydia was confused, terrified of the truth and the pain of giving birth and she felt even more alone in her journey than before.

Deep in her heart Lydia began to understand that her mother knew what was happening to her daughter all along. Lydia questioned, in the dark hour of the wolf, her mother's motives and feelings towards her. How could she let it happen?

Many years later, at Christmas 2014, Harriet visited Lydia at her new home in the UK. Lydia was married with a nine-year-old son, whom she adored. Harriet sat with her daughter at the kitchen table enjoying some of the fermented prune juice she had brought from Spain, and she decided that it was time for Lydia to find out some more details about the past.

That was the moment Harriet, after one too many glasses of *tuica*, opened her mouth and looked Lydia in the eyes.

'My dearest Lydia, I am so sorry about what had happened to you.'

Lydia looked at her mother. Past experience told her to keep quiet, to wait for Harriet to continue. Lydia waited patiently for Harriet to speak again.

'Sergiu told me, you know, when we decided to get married, that if you were a girl, I had to keep you away from him because of his condition.' Lydia was completely taken aback.

'What do you mean?' she managed to ask, from the fogginess of the alcohol and the revelation which opened up the subject for a much deeper understanding.

Beginnings

'Your father told me that he liked little girls, my dear,' answered Harriet, 'and he did not want me to live with him and bring you with me.'

This is how Lydia finally discovered the truth about her mother's behaviour and saw Harriet for who she truly was. Thirty years after delivering a baby girl in the cold hospital on the outskirts of Bucharest. Words fell short of expressing what was going through Lydia's mind, heart, and body after Harriet's revelation. She kept her composure and decided to store the news and observe further.

But when Lydia was in labour that night, at the hospital in Bucharest, she knew nothing which would explain why her mother had behaved as she did.

Lydia only knew that she had been admitted, and she would give birth soon.

Both Sergiu and Harriet were there, they drove her from Ploiesti when her waters broke.

Lydia felt scared at the prospect of being left on her own, with strangers.

When her parents said goodbye to her and she was taken to the wards, she felt miserable, powerless, unwanted and discarded.

During the admission process, when asked who was the father of the child, Harriet answered: 'Unknown.' The look the nurse gave Lydia said more than a thousand words.

Lydia was put into a ward with at least thirty beds, full of women screaming in pain or swearing at their absent husbands for getting them pregnant and making promises into the thin air that they would never touch 'the bastard' again.

She crawled under the sheets and waited for the pain to start. Towards midnight, another woman came to share the bed with Lydia, because apparently there was a shortage, so she had to huddle in one corner in agony. She turned her back to the room and to the world and just lay there, curled into a ball, as far as she could curl, to try and ease the pain of her contractions and the anguish of her broken heart. It was morning of 19th September 1984 when Lydia was rushed into the delivery ward, placed on the table and asked by the midwife to start pushing.

Lydia pushed as hard as she could and towards the end of the afternoon, a baby girl came into the world, only to be given away as soon as she was declared fit and healthy.

Lydia did not want to have anything to do with the child. The midwife was the only person who seemed to have a heart in that cold, strange place. She took care of Lydia as much as she could. The rest of the staff looked at her with heavy judgement in their eyes. She was treated as a floozy without the morals of a 'proper girl'.

Lydia had already learned that people would only see, hear or pay attention to what they wanted. If she was considered a girl of low moral values then so be it. Lydia was sick and tired of uneducated judgements from entitled people.

The teenage Lydia who entered the hospital was not the same one who left it. And not just because the package had been delivered. But because Lydia's own and most precious gift, her humanness, had been bent to breaking point.

Beginnings

In every woman's life, the moment of giving birth to another human being is sacred, celebrated, anticipated with joy and a sense of fulfilment. The newborn baby is held and snuggled and loved, from the very moment they leave their mother's womb.

In Lydia's case she did not allow herself to get attached to a baby born out of incest. Not in the moment of delivery, not ever.

This sacrifice scarred Lydia. She did not touch the baby; she did not go and visit her in her crib in the maternity ward and she was not concerned with her upbringing. The newborn's fate had already been decided: she would be put up for adoption.

Lydia had purposedly and consciously denied herself the basic instinct of motherhood. At the age of sixteen, and for the first time since the abuse began, Lydia felt broken. After she gave birth she was delivered back to the ward, where she lay hurting and bleeding, feeling a terrible pain in her heart.

Lydia spent a week in hospital. She needed to recover from the delivery which had caused some physical damage. Yet she was young and strong. During her stay in the maternity ward, she had one persistent visitor: Sergiu.

He showed up every day, asked how she felt and reassured her that her mother and brother would be happy to see her back home, soon.

Lydia walked alongside him through the gardens and listened to what he had to say. He constantly enquired about her keeping the promise to him and she had to

Lydia's Journey

reassure him that she had not told a soul about their relationship.

The day finally came when she was ready to leave hospital. Lydia was terrified to go back to her normal life – not only because of what that meant, but mostly because she had changed completely. She appeared obedient but on the inside was full of rage and sadness and resentment. Hate occupied her heart, and she felt shattered and extremely vulnerable. Lydia lost over twenty-five kilograms after delivering her baby and she looked almost too weak to walk. But she managed, and Sergiu drove her and her mother, who came that day, back home.

When Grandma Val finally got to see her, she stood in front of Lydia unable to utter a word for a long while.

'What has happened to you, Lydia?' she finally asked. 'Are you ill?' But Lydia was not in the mood to answer any questions and she gave her grandmother the cold shoulder.

She felt that she owed an explanation to no one. If they had not been there to care for her and keep her safe, they did not deserve anything.

The same questions followed in school when she returned to class, and the headteacher, accompanied by one of the teachers, took her into her office and asked her several questions, very personal questions which soon turned into accusations. It would have been a question of expulsion if it turned out that Lydia had been pregnant and carried her pregnancy to term. Not to mention the resentment Mrs Petrescu felt, and her dismay at the thought that a

Beginnings

teenager such as Lydia could fool her, the experienced veteran of a prestigious nursing school. But Lydia could not care less for her arguments, nor her accusations. She did not answer. She did not admit. She denied any such allegations and politely invited Mrs Petrescu to mind her own business.

With no direct confession, no direct proof, no punishment could be inflicted. Lydia could not be expelled.

The classes of her third year in high school had started two weeks before Lydia was back at school, but she soon caught up and fell into the routine again.

The following months, Lydia felt as though she was broken. There was nothing but numbness in her heart and in her mind. She didn't care whether it was day or night, she ate to please her mother and grandmother, and get them off her back, but she had lost the will to live. She did not consider suicide, but she wanted to just go to bed and not wake until her nightmare was over and she was in the world she wanted: full of love, and care and joy and magic.

Months passed by quickly and Lydia slowly began her journey to recovery. She started to go to church again with Grandma Val. She enjoyed the peace and quiet of the place, and in the years that followed she finally made peace with Jesus in her heart. She could not give up hope. She had to keep it alive – the hope that one day she would be free. Trust she had lost but hope, she could not part with that.

Lydia's Journey

Lydia attended a second autopsy at the invitation of her teacher. That time, only three of her fellow students showed up and Lydia got to witness the process in its entirety. She stood there from the beginning, surrounded by her colleagues and several first year residents and when Lydia looked around the room she was shocked to realise it was devoid of emotion. There he was, a sixteen-year-old boy dead on the table, his remains were about to be opened and investigated, and not a single person in that room paid attention to his body with the respect and reverence Lydia thought he deserved. Her colleagues were smoking – yes, back then in 1984, one was allowed to smoke in a hospital in Romania – and chatting and touching the organs and measuring them and writing down numbers and conclusions. Lydia felt sick to her stomach. She wanted to leave the room and run outside, into the sunlight. Maybe it was because she was the same age as the corpse on the table, or maybe it was because she took the lack of respect as a denial of the humanness in that body which had once belonged to a person; the same lack of reverence she had recently been shown by people who didn't even care about her circumstances nor how she felt.

In that moment, Lydia felt alive again, full of spark and ready to face the next chapter in her life. She understood that the open body in front of her had no more choices, unlike Lydia who did have them, and would do for as long as she drew breath.

She looked at the boy on the table and nearly cried. She thanked him, someone she never knew but who had taught her that life is to be appreciated and celebrated. The potential of each moment, the beauty in every instant, the perfection of every second, that is what Lydia had taken

Beginnings

from her second and last session in that autopsy room.

As difficult as it was for Lydia to admit, given her intense desire to follow a medical career, she had to consider whether she was cut out to be a doctor.

Lydia had to accept that for the past several months her faith in her ability to learn had been somewhat shaken. She was extremely emotional, and everything seemed to either bother her or trigger tears. She hoped that in time, she would recover and find solace in her daily routine, like she used to.

She had to find it in herself the ability to establish a routine. But how does one, resume the thread, pretend to live a normal life, when the thread had been broken? How does one come to terms with what has happened in order to survive the trauma and keep their sanity alive? Lydia had no answers. She only knew that dawn signalled the day was about to begin, nightfall meant it was about to end. She only had the here and now – that was all she could count on.

Immersed in the present, Lydia put one step in front of the other and managed to rekindle the resemblance of a routine after she gave birth and returned to school.

How does the saying go, 'The show must go on?'

Days moved into weeks which moved into months, taking Lydia further and further away from that day in a cold room and a hospital bed.

And when least expected, one day, in December 1985, Sergiu announced that he had been offered a position as a cellist in one of Spain's symphonic orchestras. He would

Lydia's Journey

be gone by next summer, he announced with a wide grin.

To Lydia, it felt like a miracle. Truly.

Sergiu left for Spain in June 1986 and Lydia could not have been happier about it. She went back to doing her homework in her parents' bedroom, and she started to get better grades than the previous year. Valery visited the family home again and it seemed for a while that Lydia had rediscovered her balance.

Uncle Marvin had married his lady friend Dorena who had twin boys from a previous marriage, and he moved in with her and the children, in a nice house opposite the hospital where Lydia had been born.

Once her father left, Lydia was able to see Maribel again and she could spend some time with her at her house now and then.

Lydia loved this newfound freedom. Life seemed to be returning to a kind of normality.

Before Sergiu left he took Lydia for a walk in the nearby fields. He pulled a packet of cigarettes from his pocket, opened it and offered one to Lydia. She was shocked. She didn't want to touch it for fear of it being a trap. But her father insisted, and it seemed safe. Since her stay at the hospital, Sergiu had treated her more as a romantic partner than an abused daughter. He tried to appear charming and compassionate, full of the patronising exquisiteness of a predator. Lydia concluded that he was a deeply disturbed and dangerous man.

She went along, holding the cigarette between her fingers, and waited for the outcome.

Beginnings

'I'll be gone soon, Lydia, and I would like to make sure that you will remain the same girl I have been watching over for the last eight years.'

With a flicker of his fingers, Sergiu lit the cigarette then passed the lighter to Lydia, gesturing for her to do the same.

'I wanted you to have your first cigarette with me, in case next time we meet you had already started to smoke. You do come from a family of smokers … Just make sure it is quality tobacco, it tastes better,' he added.

Lydia looked at him and nodded. She had never thought of smoking before, until that moment when she was offered a cigarette by her father.

Years later, in therapy, she understood what motivated this action, along with everything else: it was to prove his power over her. Even when he was far away he would be able to have control over her thoughts, through fear.

But finally he left. Lydia felt free. She had not forgotten that her mother was informing him of what was going on in his absence so Lydia made sure to keep things low key. She did muster the courage to ask her father in a letter if he would allow her to wear the silver ring her grandmother Maria – Sergiu's mother – had given her as a gift, before he left.

'Just because I am gone, it doesn't mean I have changed my view on jewellery,' he wrote back.

Not yet, Lydia, she told herself. *Not yet*.

Lydia's Journey

Shortly after her husband left Harriet got a contract with the same philharmonic orchestra in Spain. She had a few months to bring her classical music skills back into her fingers, therefore she started to rehearse. She had been out of practice for over sixteen years, and she became nervous about her ability to play again.

Lydia could not believe her luck. She would be left behind to care for her brother until her parents obtained travel visas for them both. Based on her previous experience of 'being reunited with the family', and how long it actually took, Lydia began to dream big. She didn't say a word to anybody.

The festive season that year was more joyful than ever. Marvin had invited his sister and her children to spend Christmas at his house, with his new wife and all of their children. Dorena had given birth that year to a beautiful baby girl, the third biological child of Uncle Marvin and his fifth in total. The family was very happy with the new arrival.

At New Year 1986 Lydia laughed, danced and giggled with her cousins in the kitchen, sneaking to get some desserts, and played with them and their little sister in Uncle Marvin's bedroom.

Lydia still remembers with a grin how one of her twin step cousins, Alvin, found a funny-looking latex balloon in his stepdad's bedside table and, disregarding its odd shape, blew into it. When Lydia looked closer, she understood what Alvin was holding in his hand and she told him. Lydia could not contain her deep, belly laughter and she bent double at his reaction.

That night was one of the best ever, Lydia told herself,

Beginnings

and she felt a fuzzy, warm feeling in her heart on their drive back to the apartment.

Harriet left for Spain in June 1987. That summer Lydia enjoyed the sunshine and the beaches at the Black Sea without the ever presence of her parents. It felt such a relief to be able to walk and talk, and even think, without their constant censuring.

As summer was coming to an end, Valery received a phone call from the college's headteacher to enlist Lydia in the grape harvest at a nearby vineyard. She was requested to be in the schoolyard in two days' time, with a small suitcase, holding enough clothing to last her for two weeks. Lydia would live and eat on site and share a bedroom with her classmates. It would be her first ever time outside the family environment and Lydia was a little nervous. She had never gone to summer camps or sleepovers.

Lydia did as she was told and soon found herself climbing onto the bus parked in front of the school building, waiting in anticipation of a new experience.

When they arrived at the vineyards, about a forty-five minute bus ride from Ploiesti, Lydia found herself in the middle of kilometres and kilometres of vines, fields, and open, blue sky.

The following morning, they all got up before dawn and went outside to have breakfast with the rest of the group. Lydia had never worked as part of a team before, except in PE when they would play ball games. To be sitting at a large table on a dusty patio with other thirty or so

Lydia's Journey

students was new to her and a bit overwhelming. She lacked the ability to make small talk. She had forgotten how to relate to her peers. She had a genuinely open mind and inquisitive curiosity, yet throughout the years her parents had encouraged her shyness and in that moment, at that big table, she felt uncomfortable.

The instructors waiting for them in the fields taught them how to harvest the grapes with minimum damage to the fruit. They were all assigned rows and left on their own until lunchtime. The bell rang and they were called back to the table for a meal, before being sent back out to the fields.

The grapes were delicious, especially in the morning, and although they were sprayed with pesticides, Lydia couldn't resist them.

She only lasted three days at the vineyards. She didn't feel comfortable, she did not know how to behave amongst her peers. She knew how to pretend in school, for several hours at a time, but here in the open, with so many hours spent with the same people, she felt lost and did not like it. She decided to flee.

She spoke with the cooks, three nice ladies living in the village nearby, and asked for their assistance. They smiled at her and told her she would not be the first one. Every year, during harvest season, students attempted to escape from the grounds. Some succeeded, others got caught.

Lydia decided to try anyway.

That night Lydia waited for her roommates to go to dinner. When the dorms seemed to be empty, Lydia snuck her small suitcase through the window, where one of her accomplices from the kitchen was waiting. She took the

Beginnings

suitcase and Lydia followed shortly, sliding down past the windowsill.

It was dark and they made sure to keep in the shadows until they reached the outskirts of the camp. They bordered the village's cemetery. A shiver ran down Lydia's spine as she was walked through the silent graves, but they made it through with no ghost or similar spooking them.

Lydia thanked the ladies then headed off to the bus station about a thirty-minute walk away, to catch the last bus to Ploiesti. She arrived in her home town well past 1 a.m. She then took another local bus and arrived at Valery's apartment around an hour later. She knocked at the door and her grandma peered through a crack, before she opened it widely to receive her.

'What are you doing here?' asked Valery. 'Did you run away? Oh, dear Lord, you are going to be in so much trouble!' But she gave Lydia a long hug and thanked God for keeping her safe.

When Lydia's last year of college started, her grandma would have to attend a meeting with the headteacher to discuss Lydia's plan of redemption. A formal apology and several bags of quality coffee seemed to satisfy an angry Mrs Petrescu. Lydia managed to bribe her way out of a more serious punishment for her conduct.

This last year turned out to be harder than Lydia had expected.

When Harriet left for Spain Grandma Val moved in with the Munteanu children.

And some weeks after the school year started, Lydia suffered a major breakdown, which she tried to sort out on her own.

Lydia's Journey

Before Sergiu left for Spain, he made sure that Lydia had a private tutor during her last year at Nursing College. Mrs Galvan was a retired pharmacist with a reputation of excellence gained over her many years of tutoring hundreds of students who had successfully been admitted into the medical school in Bucharest, the crème de la crème, the best of the best.

From the beginning of September 1986, Lydia started her programme with Mrs Galvan. Twice weekly, Lydia would go to her house after school and spend hours learning, writing and going through hundreds of mock exams.

Soon school became too overwhelming for Lydia, and she refused to go. Not openly, of course, but she could not cope with it. She would get up in the morning and get ready as usual, only she would go to Valery's apartment and sleep in her bed, until she knew she had to be back home. She returned, pretending to have been in school. This lasted for about three weeks, until Uncle Marvin came one morning to Valery's apartment in search of her. Mrs Galvan had told him about Lydia not attending her weekly private lessons and he couldn't find her anywhere. He was, however, a good substitute father to Lydia, in the sense that he did not want Valery to find out and complicate things. He and Lydia discussed the issue and Lydia had to go back to school, catch up on all her missed nursing practice and on all her missed homework.

So she did.

Mrs Galvan had reminded Lydia of her potential in memorising and learning, reigniting her competitive spirit. And Lydia did her best because, secretly, she was praying for her parents never to send her that travel visa for Spain, and that she would in fact get to attend a university in Romania.

Beginnings

Mrs Galvan was extremely pleased with Lydia's high scores in all her mock tests and she had no doubt that Lydia would be one of her prize students by the end of the year. And Lydia felt confident in herself again.

A couple of months before her mother left for Spain, Harriet had sat Lydia down to talk to her.

'I will be leaving soon, Lydia, and you will be in charge of your little brother,' she announced solemnly. Lydia already knew that, but her mother was not finished.

'We will get you and Liviu out of the country as soon as possible, it will hopefully be no more than a couple of months,' Harriet said.

Lydia knew from previous experience that a couple of months might turn into at least a couple of years. She wasn't concerned. She knew that with her mother gone, Lydia would have the freedom to do what she wanted: pass her exams and be admitted to the medical school in Bucharest.

'Continue with the private lessons, Lydia, but it will be just for show. If they find out that we plan to take you with us to Spain you and Liviu will be thrown out of school, so you have to make sure that doesn't happen,' her mother continued.

'What do you mean?' asked Lydia astonished.

'I mean that if you let anybody know that your father and I are planning to take you out of the country too, then your schools will not allow you to continue your studies. You will not be able to pursue any university degree without your college degree so you will have to be very careful when you talk to people about us, and about your plans.'

Lydia's Journey

Instantly, Lydia was reminded of her first day of school, when she was made to feel guilty for the treachery of her parents who had dared to leave the country in search of a better life in a democratic regime.

Lydia could not catch a break. But she decided that she would continue to study with the same enthusiasm and effort anyway, because she secretly hoped that her parents would never ask her to join them to Spain.

At the end of college, as it is customary, they organised a ball.

But this was not just any ball. It would be held in a restaurant at a hotel in Sinaia, a posh sought-after holiday destination outside Ploiesti. It was also a historical site, where the eighteenth-century kings of Romania built Peles Castle as their summer residence.

The city was absolutely enchanting. Whitewashed villas with pointed red roofs designed to withstand the harsh snows in the winter, were set against the mountain slopes. Some were barely visible through the treetops in the summer, others were situated by the bank of the river with its crystalline waters that ran through the middle of town. The parks and promenades inspired an imaginative mind to create the ambience of a European mid-eighteenth-century lifestyle. The entire town and its officials had made it their mission to preserve the unadulterated beauty and history of Sinaia and this quiet village at the foot of a mountain, became an internationally-renowned tourist site in Europe.

And it was here that the Class of 1987 Ploiesti Nursing College Prom was held.

Beginnings

Lydia had made it through the four years, and she needed to let her hair down. Since her class was ninety percent female, the headteacher decided to invite a male-based year from another college in Ploiesti.

Before the event, the two schools got together so the students could socialise and get to know each other a little bit before the Prom. Lydia did not like strangers looking through the windows of her classroom or launching glances her way as she walked down the corridor. Some even wanted to talk to her but she was too conditioned to allow herself such an exchange.

She attended the ball but wore an outfit which ensured no one would ask her to dance. It was a two-piece, three-quarter length, white ensemble, with the blouse hanging below her waist line and over the skirt. It made her look like a barrel with feet. She spent the dinner talking to another girl who was just as antisocial as she was when it came to dancing or relating to other young adults. That night Lydia understood how different she was from all the other girls in the room, and she felt emotionally stunted. She was embarrassed about her dress, her hair, her manners. She felt fake and exposed. She became acutely aware of her lack of social skills, and she wished she had never come. It did not feel like a celebration to Lydia, it was more like a humiliation. The most difficult moment of that night was when Lydia began to understand that she had had no say in the way she had become. She had not been allowed to develop her own personality, rather she was the person she had been told she should be. The gap in Lydia's emotional development in comparison to her peers was embarrassingly obvious.

When the last goodbye had been said and the academic year had come to an end, Lydia had to tell Mrs Galvan the

Lydia's Journey

truth about her and Liviu leaving for Spain when their travel visas arrived. Even if she wanted to, Lydia could not pretend to take a university degree in Romania any longer. Her tutor looked genuinely sad and disappointed. Lydia could see it in her eyes.

The days began to drag until one day, out of nowhere, one of her father's former cello students found his way to Lydia's apartment and offered her a gift, 'intended to cheer you up until you are reunited with your parents.' The man stood in the doorway of the apartment holding a beautifully-wrapped object. Lydia did not know how to react. She felt curious about the gift but wary about the way in which it was presented. Lydia had never had a boyfriend, nor did she know how to react to the offering. She declined it and shut the door in his face. She had a fearful feeling in the pit of her stomach. Fear of her father, who would punish her for accepting gifts from a stranger. And then came guilt, when Lydia realised that her refusal of his kind gesture must have been hurtful. Shame followed and Lydia was at a loss. When she understood how rude she had been, when she realised that she had refused an opportunity to experience something so foreign to her, she could not resist the temptation of having a real boyfriend.

He was four years older than Lydia and seemed to be a nice person. Lydia wanted some company so she agreed to go out with him.

At first, it felt surreal. She was nineteen years old and he was her first boyfriend. His name was Lukas.

Grandma Val did not like Lukas. Valery and Uncle Marvin hinted to Lydia that he was not truly in love with

Beginnings

her; rather he was interested in leaving the country with Lydia if she could convince her parents that her feelings towards him were true.

But Lydia had had enough of other people telling her what to feel or think and although she felt hurt by those comments, she decided to go ahead and see for herself what a real relationship meant.

They went to the cinema, they held hands and took long walks through parks, they talked and laughed and kissed.

That was all new to Lydia. Lukas was Lydia's first hand hold, first kiss, first male companion with whom she shared laughter and ideas. Being with him seemed to have washed away her sins, or what she considered to be her sins. She liked the contact with his lips, they were soft and inviting. He asked her to sit with him at the museum where her mother used to work, where he rented a small room for his private guitar and violin students.

Lukas played the classical guitar wonderfully. Lydia loved to watch him play and listen to the sound of the instrument vibrating beneath his fingertips. Soon enough Lukas offered to teach her.

Little by little, Lukas found his way to her heart and Lydia spent more and more time in his company. She had no school to attend and no prospects in this country. She waited for their visas to come through and during this time fell in love with Lukas.

He was slender, athletic and taller than Lydia. He wore his blond hair in a stylish haircut and had a slanted smile which Lydia found attractive.

Lukas invited her to meet his parents, Martin and Sylvia, and she discovered they lived close to the boulevard where her family had first rented an apartment on their return from Germany.

Martin and Sylvia lived on the top floor of a tall building. Lukas had a younger sister, Anna, and an even younger brother, Samuel. His parents seemed nice people and Lydia felt welcome. She started visiting them more often. They loved to play board games and Lydia was soon included.

Lukas' family also owned a house in town which they kept for personal use, rather than rent it out. Once or twice Lukas stopped to pick something up from there, and that was how Lydia found out where it was.

On one occasion Lukas invited Lydia to spend the afternoon at the house. They agreed a day and time and Lydia considered what this meant. She had two days until the date, in which she had to decide what to do. She found it impossible to bypass the fear of her father or the sarcasm of her mother, if she gave in to Lukas. She feared the label of 'whore' they would give her if she met with Lukas that afternoon. So Lydia sent him a handwritten note, via a mutual friend, in which she let him know that she was not ready. Lukas seemed to be OK with her decision. He never pushed her, never asked her anything about it.

It was the beginning of December 1987, when Lukas showed up at her door in distress and asked her if she had seen his brother. Lydia had not.

'Would you mind coming to help me find him?' asked Lukas.

'Of course,' said Lydia, sensing his unease.

Beginnings

They both went to friends' houses, walked through town, spent the entire day looking for Samuel. He was sixteen years old and was nowhere to be found. The last time he had been seen was two days earlier.

'Mum, I couldn't find him,' said Lukas over the phone to his mother. 'I don't know where else to look.' He hung up.

'Let's go back to the house, Mum mentioned something about him going there before he left the apartment.' So off they went.

Lukas went in first and when Lydia followed him inside, a faint smell of something sweet and rotten greeted her at the entrance. Perhaps a small bird was trapped in the fireplace, and Lydia went over to take a look while Lukas busily searched through the house.

As he walked up the stairs Lydia was just about to follow, when he turned around and stopped her.

'No, stay here, Lydia, I don't want to leave the front door unattended.' She walked into the kitchen and was about to pour herself a glass of water when she heard a scream of terror from the attic. Lydia started running towards him, but Lukas blocked her way.

'Call the police, now, Lydia,' he shouted, 'Don't go in there, please, call the police.' Lydia saw horror in his eyes.

She walked back downstairs and rang the police from the house phone. Lukas joined her in the living room.

'Samuel is upstairs, in the attic … He … he … h-h-h-hung himself.' Lukas broke down in tears, his entire body shaking. Lydia's heart skipped a beat. She went over to hug Lukas, and he crumpled in her arms. He was a dead weight and she could barely support him, but she wanted to be there for him so held him until the police came.

Lydia's Journey

Two policemen and a coroner arrived and went into the attic. As they finally came down the stairs Lydia was afraid to look. From the corner of her right eye she saw a white bedsheet carrying the body – an arm hung down – and she and Lukas had to leave the house. Lydia did not know what to do. It was late but she didn't feel like she could leave Lukas alone.

He walked her home and asked her to wait for him to phone her. He had to break the news to his parents and sister and the police also wanted him to go to the station.

Lydia said goodbye and went inside. Valery was waiting for her, angry at her lack of punctuality. Lydia had completely forgotten that she had promised her grandma she would be home by 8 p.m. It was past 10 p.m. But when Lydia told Valery why she was late her grandma crossed her chest and said a prayer for Samuel's soul.

They went to the kitchen and spent some time talking. Lydia could not go to bed and Valery understood. Having lost a son herself, Valery showed compassion towards Samuel and they both felt very sad that night. It was well past midnight when they finally went to bed and Lydia asked her grandma if she could sleep with her. Valery agreed.

The following days were heartbreaking. Lukas looked like a ghost when she next saw him, the day of Samuel's funeral. It was a short ceremony and his parents managed to have him buried in sacred ground, despite his act of suicide, which the orthodox church regarded as an unforgiveable sin.

From that day onwards, Lukas permeated an air of sadness. Understandably. And Lydia was the shoulder for him to cry on. Also, understandable, and somehow, predictable.

Beginnings

Just before Lydia's twentieth birthday she was given the news that their visas had arrived. Lydia and Liviu would be departing in February 1988.

Lydia understood that she would now have to stand up for herself and tell Grandma Val and Uncle Marvin that she had decided to stay in the country, prepare for her admission exams in Bucharest and live her life in Romania. She knew it would be a difficult argument to win, but she hoped that her newfound relationship with Lukas would soften her uncle's stance.

Lydia invited Uncle Marvin to her parents' apartment. They sat in the kitchen sipping coffee and smoking cigarettes – Sergiu was right, Lydia had taken up smoking after Harriet's departure. Lydia asked her uncle to understand and support her in her decision to remain in the country.

They spoke about what staying would be like, about Lydia's prospects for the future, about the financial aspect of staying behind and, above all, about the foolishness of such a decision. Uncle Marvin did listen to Lydia, and to a certain point he even sympathised with her feelings towards Lukas, but when she began to talk about her desire to stay, he had to stop her.

'It is foolish,' he said, 'you are denying yourself the chance of a better life.'

From his perspective, living off the scraps of monthly rationed staples such as oil, vinegar, sugar, flour; having to wake up 2 a.m. to stand in the queue for half a kilogram of chicken legs and wings, or for two loaves of rationed bread; following the rules of a political regime with the supreme power to end life with a snap of the fingers, was not living. And for Marvin, the fact that Lydia was giving

Lydia's Journey

up on a life with the potential to achieve her dreams, in the name of love, was simply unacceptable.

'I am truly sorry, Lydia, but I cannot and I will not support your request. It is absurd.'

Lydia could not tell him the real reason behind her wish. How could she?

And that was the end of it.

Lydia was a regular presence at Lukas' parents' place, more so after the death of Samuel. She found that her being there was soothing to them, and it was also of comfort to her.

Valery and Marvin were not in favour of these visits and once or twice they showed up at Lukas' apartment and requested Lydia came home with them. And she did. But it was humiliating. Lydia was almost twenty years old.

One morning, after a fight with her grandmother, Lydia felt something inside her snap. The tension was too much. Valery was clearly afraid that Lydia would give up the opportunity of a brighter future for the sake of Lukas and she felt it was her responsibility to keep Lydia on the right path.

Lydia remembered her father's medication stash and went through the drugs in search of diazepam.

Wouldn't it be nice, thought Lydia, *to fall asleep and wake up when all this nonsense, and tension and mess is over?* Rhetorical question, of course, but Lydia was so tired and emotionally drained, that it was a great thought. She took one 5mg tablet of diazepam. After about 30 minutes Lydia could not feel anything from the drug, so she decided to

Beginnings

take another one. Another half an hour, no effects. So she took two more. And then, ten minutes later, she took another two pills.

Just when she was about to take even more, Lukas called and asked her to meet with him. She travelled by bus from her apartment to his.

Lukas was waiting by the bus station for her – Lydia liked his gentlemenly manners – and when he bent over to kiss her, he stopped and looked at her closely .

'What is going on? he asked. 'Are you alright?' Lydia appreciated the concern about her in his eyes.

'I'm fine, Lukas, just a bit tired,' said Lydia.

They left the bus station holding hands.

When they arrived at his parents', the table was already prepared for dinner – Lukas' mum was a good cook – and then they would play some board games.

After they had eaten Lydia started to feel tired. They had just started a game of canasta but Lydia could not keep her eyes open, and she asked for permission to take a nap.

'Are you feeling OK, honey? asked Sylvia.

'Just a bit tired,' said Lydia and she retired to their bedroom to lay on the bed.

She was woken by a pair of hands, shaking her shoulders, and a voice she did not recognise at first, calling her name. It was Lukas. She opened her eyes, with difficulty, and when she looked at him through the fog of her recent sleep, she noticed that it was dark and the streetlights from below were shining into the room.

'What time is it?' asked Lydia.

Lydia's Journey

'It's almost ten o'clock. Your grandma just called ... I'm really sorry, Lydia, but you will have to go, I don't want her to come knocking at the door again, my parents have been through a lot already.' Lukas looked sad and embarrassed about what he had just said.

Lydia looked at him, kissed his cheek and stood up to get ready to leave. She felt dizzy when she rose, but it soon passed. She started walking and felt unsecure on her feet. She reached out for support and found the wall. The room seemed really dark.

As she said goodbye to Lukas' parents and sister, she sensed concern for her wellbeing in Sylvia's eyes.

'Are you sure you're OK?' she asked again, but Lydia reassured her that everything was fine and she left with Lukas.

He waited with her until her bus arrived then kissed her goodbye.

'Call me when you get home,' he said before the doors of the bus closed and it started to move. The bus seemed really dark. Lydia felt as though it was spinning, and she did not remember too much from the journey.

When she finally arrived home, her grandma was there to receive her. She took one look at Lydia, held back any comments, and went to the kitchen to put the coffee machine on. Lydia thought it was a miracle. She had expected all hell to break loose and instead, she was greeted with coffee. She could not focus her eyes and her speech was sluggish. She was unable to articulate her words properly and the light in the hallway and the kitchen appeared particularly bright.

'Come on, dear,' said Grandma, 'let's sit down and have

Beginnings

this cup of coffee together.' She pulled the chair over for Lydia to sit.

Her brother then walked into the apartment and after talking to somebody in the hallway, he closed and locked the front door behind him.

'Liviu,' said Valery, 'pull up a chair and join us.'

What is going on, why is everybody being so nice? wondered Lydia. But she kept her thoughts to herself and started sipping her coffee.

It was delicious and she asked for another cup.

Grandma poured some more and when she considered that Lydia would be OK, she left her in Liviu's care and went to bed. After all, it was past 2 a.m. and Grandma was in her seventies.

After Valery left, her brother explained why their grandmother had acted as she did that night.

Lukas had phoned the apartment asking if Lydia had arrived home and Valery told him that Lydia was not back yet. Then a friend of Valery's called to inform them that Lydia had just paid her a visit asking to spend the night there as she was afraid of her grandmother. Valery's friend declined this request and Lydia had left, in the friend's opinion, looking and acting drunk, unsteady on her feet and inarticulate.

In the meantime, Lukas had showed up at the apartment and he and Liviu had gone to look for Lydia, to make sure she had not fallen on her way back from the bus station to the apartment.

'Was it Lukas you were speaking to when you arrived home tonight?' asked Lydia.

Lydia's Journey

'Yes, it was Lukas,' said Liviu

And it was also Lukas who had told Valery and Liviu to keep Lydia awake when she arrived home, to not let her sleep until she acted normally. He told them to give Lydia coffee and spend the night with her.

'Lukas cares about you,' said Liviu and Lydia knew it to be true.

Lydia recovered from the incident with no side effects. She was afraid for a while that the tablets might affect her memory, and was relieved when it became clear that they hadn't.

Uncle Marvin threw a party for Lydia's twentieth birthday as her gift. It was held at his house, and everybody had fun that evening. Everybody but Lydia.

Liviu was excited to leave Romania . During their last months there Lydia had to sell all their belongings, her precious book collection, absolutely everything other than her and her brother's clothes.

The two months before her departure she would see Lukas every day, they would spend many hours together. On their last meeting Lukas just wanted to hold Lydia's hands and sit in silence. She respected his wish and they sat, tucked into one another on the bench, in a park covered in fresh snow, silently holding hands. Lydia's head leaned against his shoulder and she cried softly. Lukas was crying too.

Then he took her home, kissed her goodbye, quickly, so as to not give into more tears, and pulled away from her abruptly. That would be the last time Lydia ever saw or spoke to Lukas.

Beginnings

The next morning came quickly and Lydia, Liviu and Grandma Val got into Marvin's car and headed for the airport.

Lydia remembered her last trip to an airport. In a land in ruins, with a heavy, broken heart.

Not much different to how she felt in that moment.

At least Harriet, who had divorced Sergiu as soon as she arrived in Spain, had reassured Lydia that both Liviu and Lydia would be staying with her. From what Harriet told them in her phone calls, the place she lived was wonderful: full of palm trees, hot in the summer, warm in the winter, with beaches as far as the eye can see and blue sea waters. It sounded lovely, and Lydia took solace in that. At least she would be living far away from her father Lydia told herself, even though they would be in the same country.

When they arrived at the airport and went to customs, each of them carrying two suitcases with their belongings, the officer, a stocky lady with a stern face looked at their passports and their travel visas.

'I need to see the luggage visa', she said.

'I don't know what you mean?' Lydia muttered.

The woman looked at her. 'The luggage visa, you have to have a luggage visa if you want to carry more than one suitcase to the plane.'

Lydia looked at her dumbstruck. And then she looked at Valery and Marvin. Both stood there shocked: nobody had told them anything about such a visa.

Lydia's Journey

'Well,' said the woman impatiently.

'I'm afraid I didn't know anything about it,' mumbled Lydia, fearing the worst.

'I can't let you go with four suitcases,' the customs officer replied. 'You'll have to leave three behind,' and she looked at the passenger behind Lydia in the queue.

'Next!'

As quickly as she could, Lydia unpacked all her belongings, right there in the busy airport, sorting through her and her brother's essentials. She packed them tightly in the biggest suitcase she was carrying and approached the counter again.

This time she was allowed to pass, and she turned to hug her grandma and Uncle Marvin. Liviu did the same then they started walking down the corridor, towards the international area.

She looked back once more before they disappeared from sight, and she waved them goodbye.

Lydia, sitting quietly at her kitchen table, had to stop and pull herself out of her memories with a jolt. It seemed like an old broken record, stuck in the same groove, playing over and over again the same couple of words: 'Good bye. Good bye. Good bye.' Endlessly. And yet, she reminded herself, leaving loved ones behind might have been her motivation in finding her way back to them. Or was that precise dynamic what kept her stuck in the cycle of the same emotions? She couldn't say. But she decided to unwind the film in her mind's eye until its last photogram

Beginnings

as it felt deeply in her heart that it was the only way to make peace with her memories and the people long gone from them.

⁂

The flight to Spain was uneventful, and they landed in Madrid at midday on the 20th February 1988. Lydia told Liviu to follow her and they passed through customs, through the international zone and finally through arrivals where they looked for Harriet waving at them.

But Harriet was not there. Lydia looked and walked around and looked again. Everywhere. So did Liviu. But their mother was nowhere to be seen.

Lydia had no mobile phone; she could not call her mother anyway as she didn't know her number. Nor her father's. Not that she would have wanted to speak to him. They could do nothing else but wait. She carried the suitcase in one hand, held Liviu's hand tightly in the other and walked towards some available seats in the arrivals area. They sat down facing the sliding doors under the 'exit' sign and waited.

Hours passed by as Lydia and her brother watched those doors open and close, open and close. Endlessly. People rushed through them, some in, others out. Everybody seemed to be in a hurry. Then she started looking at the people waiting for their family, or friends, or business partners. It was interesting to witness such displays of emotion and this kept her entertained for a while.

Harriet was still nowhere to be seen.

Four hours passed, and Lydia started to wonder what would be the best course of action if her mother didn't show up.

Lydia's Journey

Unfortunately for Lydia she had not learned from her previous lack of perspective regarding learning the language prior to her arrival in the country. So, there she was again, with her younger brother in her charge this time, in a foreign airport, not knowing a soul and not speaking the language.

She remembered with a flashback her experience in Germany, but regrets would not solve her present predicament.

The only option was to sit and wait. And so, they did.

After what it seemed to be an eternity, Lydia saw a tall figure walking through the door, wearing a long winter coat and walking purposefully towards their seats. When she looked closer, she felt her heart jump out of her chest – it was their father, it was Sergiu.

She stood up and looked at him with a tight and tired smile and gave Liviu a little nudge to acknowledge their father's presence.

Liviu stood up and looked at his father, puzzled.

'Your mother couldn't make it today, you both are coming with me,' said Sergiu. Lydia's entire positive mindset collapsed.

The three of them walked out of the airport and towards Sergiu's car.

Welcome to Spain.

www.ingramcontent.com/pod-product-compliance
Lightning Source LLC
Chambersburg PA
CBHW030300100526
44590CB00012B/464